SERIES EDITOR: JOHN MOORE

ORDER OF BATTLE 12

THE ARDENNES OFFENSIVE

I. ARMEE & VI. ARMEE

SOUTHERN SECTOR

BRUCE QUARRIE

OSPREY
MILITARY

First published in Great Britain in 2001 by Osprey Publishing, Elms Court, Chapel Way, Botley, Oxford OX2 9LP United Kingdom
Email: info@ospreypublishing.com

ISBN 1 85532 913 1

Osprey Series Editor: Lee Johnson
Ravelin Series Editor: John Moore
Research Co-ordinator: Diane Moore
Design: Ravelin Limited, Braceborough, Lincolnshire, United Kingdom
Cartography: Chapman Bounford and Associates, London, United Kingdom
Index by Alan Rutter
Origination by Magnet Harlequin, Uxbridge, United Kingdom
Printed in China through World Print Ltd

01 02 03 04 05   10 9 8 7 6 5 4 3 2 1

FOR A CATALOGUE OF ALL BOOKS PUBLISHED BY OSPERY MILITARY AND AVIATION PLEASE WRITE TO:
The Marketing Manager, Osprey Direct, P.O. Box 140,
Wellingborough, Northants, NN8 4ZA, United Kingdom.
Email: info@ospreydirect.co.uk

The Marketing Manager, Osprey Direct USA,
c/o Motorbooks International, PO Box 1,
Osceola, MI 48311-0130, USA.
Email: info@ospreydirectusa.com

BUY ONLINE AT www.ospreypublishing.com

Key to Military Series symbols

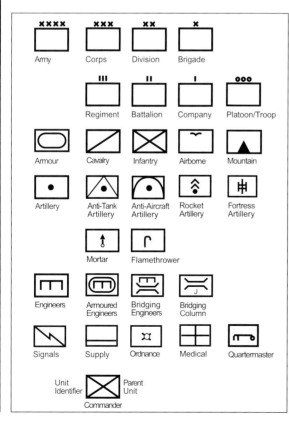

Series style

The style of presentation adopted in the Order of Battle series is designed to provide quickly the maximum information for the reader.

Order of Battle Unit Diagrams – All 'active' units in the ORBAT, that is those present and engaged on the battlefied, are shown in black. Unengaged and detached units, as well as those covered in subsequent volumes, are 'shadowed'.

Unit Data Panels – These provide a ready reference for all regiments, battalions, companies and troops forming part of each division or battlegroup and present during the battle, together with dates of attachment where relevant.

Battlefield Maps – In this volume, German units engaged are shown in red and Allied units in blue.

Order of Battle Timelines

Battle Page Timelines – Each volume concerns the Order of Battle for the armies involved. Rarely are the forces available to a commander committed into action as per his ORBAT. To help the reader follow the sequence of events, a Timeline is provided at the bottom of each 'battle' page. This Timeline gives the following information:

The top line bar defines the actual time of the actions being described in that battle section.

The middle line shows the time period covered by the whole action.

The bottom line indicates the page numbers of the other, often interlinked, actions covered in this book.

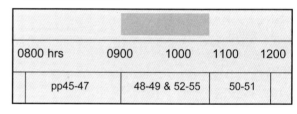

0800 hrs	0900	1000	1100	1200
	pp45-47	48-49 & 52-55	50-51	

Author's acknowledgements

For the very detailed information on the composition and strength of the Panzer and Panzergrenadier divisions, correcting many errors in previous publications and obtained through exhaustive research in the Freiburg archives, I am particularly indebted to Jeff Dugdale.

Editor's note

All individual battle maps are based on Government Survey 1:50,000 G.S. 4040 series dated 1938 and 1939, revised from aerial reconnaissance 1943, by permission of The British Library.

CONTENTS

STRATEGY IN THE WEST

Holding the Southern Shoulder

Remember 1940? Hitler was so worried about the exposed flanks of his Panzer divisions that he called a virtual halt to their rush to the Channel coast, giving the British an unlooked-for breathing space during which to evacuate the Expeditionary Force from Dunkerque. By 1944 the Führer was more sanguine about flanks, since experience had shown that if the tanks and motorised infantry could sustain their speed and momentum, the enemy would be sent reeling off-balance and the flanks of an offensive would become irrelevant.

Feldmarschall Walter Model's orders to the Panzer divisions involved in operation 'Herbstnebel' specific-ally directed them to ignore their flanks. Despite this, it was the 'shoulders' north and south of the Ardennes which worried him more than he admitted, and certainly more than the Panzer divisions' ability to cross the Meuse and strike for Bruxelles and Antwerp. In truth, Model and OKW were not too concerned about Montgomery's 21st Army Group forces to the north. By this stage of the war, they knew that 'Monty' was slow to react and often sluggish in his eventual response to a threat. Omar Bradley and, in particular, George Patton, on the other hand, were totally different characters who could be expected to take fast and furious measures against anything thrown at them.

At the beginning of the offensive, Model was therefore not too bothered (wrongly, as it proved) about Heeresgruppe B's northern 'shoulder'. Apart from the fact that it was 'Monty' up there in Holland, Sixth Panzer Armee was deploying four SS-Panzer divisions, which in theory should have been able to slice through the thin American lines on the Monschau-Losheim front like the proverbial knife through butter. In the centre, Fifth Panzer Armee was suitably equipped in manpower and matériel to look after itself – or so it was thought. The south, however, was a potential problem solely because of Patton's Third Army.

The volatile American general's rapid reaction times were well known, and the big question was whether he could react quickly enough on this

Although Brandenberger's Seventh Armee was sadly deficient in all forms of support weaponry and equipment, as well as motorised transport, its two Volks-Werfer Brigaden (8 and 18) were able to provide useful support on occasion since the rocket projectors were light enough to be manhandled and had a high rate of fire.
(U.S. Signal Corps)

occasion to prevent the assault on Courtney Hodges' First Army from achieving its objectives. Timing was everything, as usual. So, Model's problem was how to stop Patton ruining the game plan?

Resources were slender. After the Allied break-throughs around St Lô and Caen and the débâcle in the Falaise pocket, plus the Soviet onslaught into East Prussia through the Baltic states and towards the Balkans, German manpower was stretched to its utmost limit. So was the ability of the factories to cope under the weight of the strategic bombing offensive. Road and railway systems miraculously continued to function despite all Allied efforts to disrupt them, but this was little consolation to Model and others when planning 'Herbstnebel'. If Napoleon was constantly looking over his shoulder at Waterloo and wondering where Blücher (and Grouchy, of course) were, then Model's bête noir was Patton, and the question was how to fend him off?

OKW did its best, and in fact it was another miracle,

given the summer and autumn disasters of 1944, that they were able to salvage as much as they did for the 'last Blitzkrieg'. But something had to be sacrificed and, at the end of the day, that 'something' was Erich Brandenberger's Seventh Armee. Model and the other planners reckoned that all it had to do was delay Patton. No-one thought for a moment (except in front of Hitler) that it could do more than that, with just four infantry divisions and no tanks!

The one factor in Seventh Armee's favour was that, once across the river Our, its northernmost Korps (Baptist Kniess' LXXXV) would be able to use the natural east-west defensive line of the river Sûre to block a counter-attack. This was fine as far as it went – and in fact worked very successfully – but Brandenberger's orders only required him to advance as far west as Martelange. This blocked the main road (such as it was) from Luxembourg City and Arlon towards Bastogne, but left the other road from Neufchâteau to the west wide open. And, as events

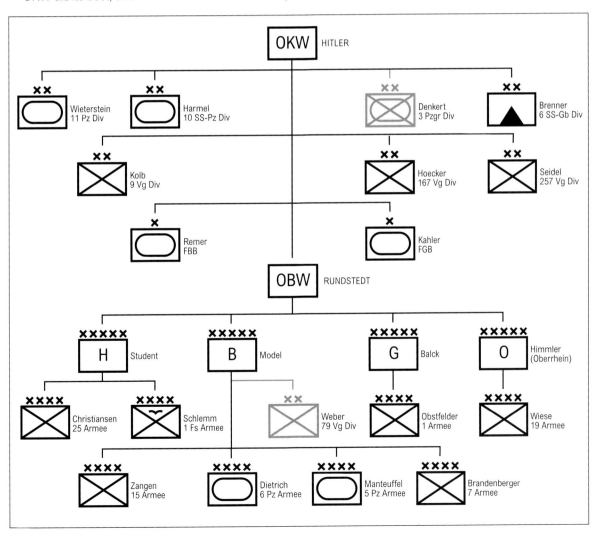

GEBIRGS DIVISION
(c. 14,000 men)

Stabs Kompanie including Landkarte Zug (c. 200 men)

GEBIRGSJÄGER REGIMENT (x2)
(Each c. 3,250 men and 4-500 horses & mules)
Stabs Kompanie including Nachrichten Zug (c. 200 men)

I, II & III Bataillonen (each c. 1,000 men)
Stabs Kompanie
1-3, 6-8 & 11-13 Kompanien (each 3 x 5cm leGrW 36,
   3 x 8cm GrW 34 & 12 x leMG 42)
4, 9 & 14 Kompanien (each 12 x sMG 42)
5, 10 & 15 Kompanien (each including Nachrichten &
   Pionier Züge) (2 x 7.5cm GebG 36 [or recoilless IG 40] &
   4 x leMG 42)
16 Kompanie (3 x 7.5cm PaK 40, 9 x 5cm PaK 38 [or, more
   usually, a mixture of anything available to replace the
   earlier 4.7cm PaK 36(t) and 3.7cm PaK 35/36] &
   4 x leMG 42)
17 Kompanie (predominantly a general support company,
   partly motorised, carrying all the kit the 'teeth' units
   needed but could not hump over mountains; unarmed
   apart from smallarms)

GEBIRGS-ARTILLERIE REGIMENT
(c. 2,500 men and 1,500-2,000 horses & mules)
Stabs Kompanie including Nachrichten Zug

I & II Abteilungen (each c. 600 men)
(Each) Stabs Kompanie & Nachrichten Zug
1, 2, 3 & 4 Batterien (each 4 x 7.5cm GebG 36 or, by this
   stage of the war, more usually IG 40, & 4 x leMG 42)

III Abteilung (c. 800 men)
Stabs Kompanie & Nachrichten Zug
5, 6 & 7 Batterien (each 4 x 10.5cm GebH 40, IG 40 or 42,
   or standard leFH 18, & 2 x leMG 42)

IV Abteilung (c. 500 men)
Stabs Kompanie & Nachrichten Zug
8 & 9 Batterien (each 4 x 15cm sIG 33 & x 2 leMG 42)

FAHRRAD (bicycle) ABTEILUNG (c. 550 men)
(Equivalent to an Aufklärungs Abteilung with 57 x
   motorcycle)
Stabs Kompanie
1 & 2 Kompanien (each 2 x 5cm leGrW 36 & 9 x leMG 42)
3 Kompanie (including Nachrichten Zug)
   (3 x 5cm PaK 38 [probably missing in Ardennes and
   replaced by Panzerschreck], 6 x 8cm GrW 34 &
   1 x leMG 42)

GEBIRGS-PANZERJÄGER ABTEILUNG (c. 600 men)
Stabs Zug
1 & 2 Kompanien (each 12 x 5cm PaK 38 & 6 x leMG 42)

GEBIRGS-PIONIER BATAILLON (mot) (c. 1,050 men)
Stabs Zug, Nachrichten Zug; 3 x Pionier Züge (each 9 x
   leMG 42);
1 x Brückengerät B & Versorgungs Kolonnen

GEBIRGS-NACHRICHTEN ABTEILUNG (c. 475 men)
Stabs Zug
1 & 2 (Fernsprech) Kompanien (each 4 x leMG 42)
3 (Funk) Kompanie (4 x leMG 42)

GEBIRGS-VERSORGUNGS ABTEILUNG (c. 2,250 men)
Stabs Kompanie
Verwaltungs Kompanie
Fleischerei Kompanie
Bäckerei Kompanie
Feldpost Kompanie
Werkstatt Kompanie (4 x leMG 42)
4-12 Transport Kolonnen
Veterinär Kompanie
2 x Sanitäts Kompanien (each 4 x leMG 42)
2 x Krankenwagen Kolonnen
Feldgendarmerie Zug

Note: Although only the 2 (Heer) and 6 SS-Gebirgs Divisions were peripherally involved in operation 'Nordwind', the inclusion of this panel concludes the data sections on late 1944 German divisions relevant to the Ardennes offensive.

turned out, it was up this road that the American 4th Armored Division finally managed to get a task force to relieve the beleaguered defenders.

One question to which there appears to be no satisfactory answer is why, since the threat from Patton was the main worry, operation 'Nordwind' was not launched at the same time as 'Herbstnebel', or within about 48 hours. This would have decisively split Patton's and Bradley's priorities. Similarly, why was the air strike codenamed 'Bodenplatte' delayed until the New Year, instead of being prepared and launched the first day the skies cleared? The C-47s airlifting

supplies into Bastogne might never have got off the ground, which could have had a drastic effect on the whole course of the second week of the campaign.

Bastogne, of course, was not a Seventh Armee objective. It was intended as a stepping stone en route to the Meuse for Manteuffel's Fifth Panzer Armee. However, as we have already seen, the obstinacy of the defence caused 2 and (130) Panzer Divisions to detour around it, and therein lies another of the many 'what ifs?' of this campaign. Holding the southern shoulder would have been made immeasurably easier without this American 'ulcer' draining the lifeblood of

'TYPICAL' PIONIER BATAILLON
(Kopfstärke [Establishment]:
Fallschirmjäger – c. 400+ officers and men;
Panzer – 862–979;
Volksgrenadier – 600-800, average 755)

Kompanien: Stab & 1-3 (Fallschirm normally only 1-2, Volksgrenadier often only 1-2)
Strength variable and proportional to battalion but Fallschirm c. 150, Panzer c. 300 and Volksgrenadier c.250

Waffen [Armament]:
Fallschirm – (in ground role, not airborne) 4 x sMG 42, 18 x leMG 42, 12 x Flammenwerfer, 4 x 8cm GrW 34 & indeterminate
  number of Panzerfaust (probably c. 12)
Panzer – 6 x sMG 42, 27(+) x leMG 42, 16-20 x Flammenwerfer & 8 x 8cm GrW 34
Volksgrenadier – 6 x sMG 42, 27 x leMG 42, 18 x Flammenwerfer, 6 x 8cm GrW 34 & (up to) 81 x Panzerfaust

Fahrzeuge [Vehicles]:
Fallschirm – Anything available or nothing; no specific establishment
Panzer – 19 x SdKfz 251 (or other half-track), 114 x truck and car & 58 x motorcycle, plus 1-2 Brückengerät J (or K)
Volksgrenadier - 91 x truck and car, 43 x motorcycle & 19 x horse-drawn (52 horses), plus 1 x Brückengerät B

The only armoured support available to Seventh Armee at the start of the offensive was the 20 assault guns of 11 Sturmgeschutz-Brigade which Brandenberger attached to 5 Fallschirm Division, LXXXV Korps. This had the furthest to travel and was expected to face the brunt of Patton's counter-attack from the south when it inevitably came. (Imperial War Museum)

the Wehrmacht. Seventh Armee forces were not directly involved in the battle for the town, but they emphatically were in the costly struggle for the villages to its south and east after Patton's III Corps hit the road.

The operations on Seventh Armee's southern flank (Beyer's LXXX Korps) consume an inordinate amount of space in American narratives, but were essentially a sideshow. Beyer's men (unlike Kniess') failed to achieve any of their objectives and only distracted fairly minimal Allied reserves. Their efforts could much more usefully have been deployed north of the river Sûre, which would have freed LXXXV Korps' 5 Fallschirm Division to sever the Neufchâteau–Bastogne highway – especially if one of the reserve

Panzer divisions or brigades had been released earlier, rather than as a mere response to the beginning of Patton's counter-attack. But Hitler, of course, believed in astrology …

Pages 8–9: **Brandenberger knew that the forces immediately facing his Seventh Armee were relatively weak, but at the same time realised that they would probably not be brushed aside easily, given the nature of the terrain and the limited mobility as well as lack of armoured backup of his own troops. The biggest problem he faced was the strong American artillery positions emplaced on high ground and able to fire with relative impunity on his bridging sites over the Our and Sauer, delaying any backup to his infantry.**

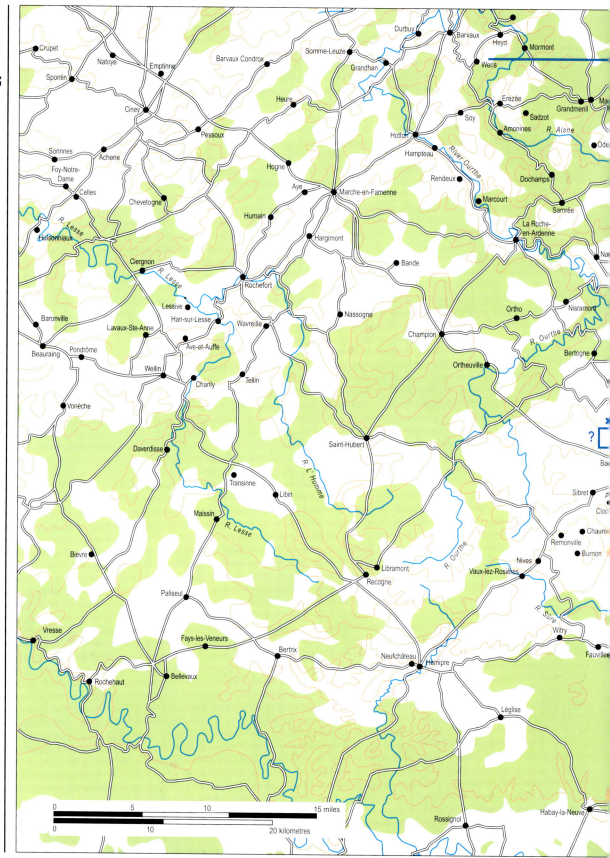

Crupet
Natoye
Emptinne
Barvaux Condrox
Somme-Leuze
Durbuy
Barvaux
Heyd
Mormont
Spontin
Grandhan
Weris
Erezée
Soy
Grandmenil
Ma
Ciney
Heure
Sadzot
Amonines
R. Aisne
Pessoux
Hotton
Ode
Sorinnes
Hampteau
Achene
Hogne
Rendeux
Dochamps
Foy-Notre-Dame
Aye
Marche-en-Famenne
Marcourt
Samrée
Celles
Chevetogne
Humain
La Roche-en-Ardenne
R. Lesse
Hargimont
Hulsonniaux
Na
Ciergnon
Bande
R. Lesse
Rochefort
Ortho
Nisramont
Lessive
Nassogne
Baronville
Han-sur-Lesse
Wavreille
R. Ourthe
Lavaux-Ste-Anne
Champlon
Bertogne
Ave-et-Auffe
Beauraing
Pondrôme
Ortheuville
Wellin
Chanly
Tellin
Vonèche
Saint-Hubert
?
Daverdisse
Ba
Transinne
R. L Homme
Sibret
Libin
Cloc
Maissin
Chaum
Remonville
R. Lesse
Burnon
Bievre
R. Ourthe
Nives
Libramont
Vaux-lez-Rosières
Recogne
Paliseul
R. Sûre
Vresse
Witry
Fays-les-Veneurs
Fauville
Bertrix
Neufchâteau
Hamipre
Rochehaut
Bellevaux
Léglise
Rossignol
Habay-la-Neuve

0 ___ 5 ___ 10 ___ 15 miles

0 ___ 10 ___ 20 kilometres

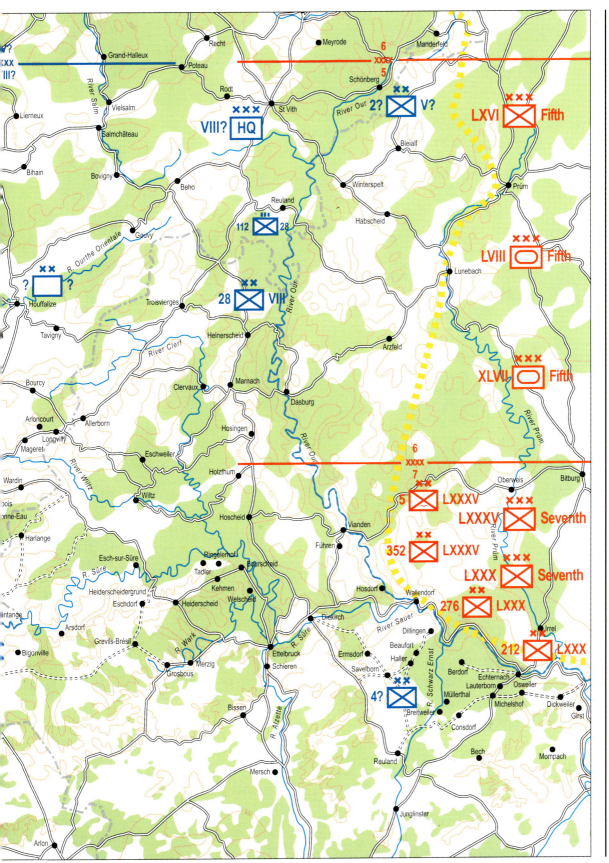

SEVENTH ARMEE

There can be little wonder in the fact that the CO of Seventh Armee, General der Panzertruppen Erich Brandenberger, was almost lost for speech when told his role in operation 'Herbstnebel'; nor that both Hasso von Manteuffel and 'Sepp' Dietrich were equally dubious about the ability of his forces to carry out their assigned mission echeloned to the left and rear of their own armies.

Model's orders for Seventh Armee's operations were explicit, as well as overly optimistic in view of Brandenberger's paucity of equipment. They stated that, 'It is the duty of the Seventh Armee to protect the flanks of the operation on the south and southwest. For this purpose, it will break through the enemy positions between Vianden and Echternach and will build up a defensive front along the line Gedinne–Libramont–Medernach.

'With the vanguard units of the Volksgrenadier divisions,' Model continued, 'the [Seventh] Armee's right wing [LXXXV Korps] will maintain contact with the Fifth Panzer Armee.' (In fact, of course, in the end it

Despite the fact that Walter Model disliked him, General der Panzertruppen Erich Brandenberger was actually a capable leader who conducted Seventh Armee's operations with great skill under very trying circumstances.
(Bundesarchiv)

was not Volksgrenadiers but Fallschirmjäger who formed 'the right wing' and over-enthusiasm led them into not only 'maintaining contact' with Manteuffel's troops, but also interfering in some of their operations, as in the battle for Wiltz, resulting in an even greater than usual 'fog of war'.)

'By energetic thrusts to the south and southwest,'

SEVENTH ARMEE

General der Panzertruppen Erich Brandenberger
Stabschef: Oberst i.G. Rudolf von Gersdorff

LXXXV Korps (Kniess)
LXXX Korps (Beyer)
LIII Korps (Rothkirch)
501 schwere Panzerjäger Abteilung (Festungs)
657 & 668 Panzerjäger Abteilungen (mot.Z)
406 & 408 Volks-Artillerie Korps
7, 15 & 16 Volks-Werfer Brigaden
660 schwere Artillerie Batterie
1092, 1093, 1124 & 1125 schwere Haubitze-Artillerie Batterien
1029, 1039 & 1122 schwere Mörser Batterien
15 Flak Regiment
44 Festungs-Machinengewehr Bataillon
XIII/999 Festungs-Infanterie Bataillon
47 Pionier Brigade (mot)
677 Bau-pionier Bataillon
961, 964, 965 & 966 Brückenkolonnen (B)
974 Brückenkolonne (J)
1 Brigade, Organization Todt (2 regiments)

Model wrote cheerfully, 'using any favourable opportunities, [Seventh Armee] will gain time and ground in order to build up a strong defensive front, carrying out intensive destruction and minelaying in front of its lines. The most important task in this connection is the destruction of the enemy artillery units stationed in front of the southern wing around Altrier.'

Finally, Model added, totally ignoring the fact that Seventh Armee was almost totally bereft of such, 'It will be necessary to provide fully adequate matériel and units for blocking purposes, as well as anti-tank weapons.' This was a tall order for the 'poor country cousin' of Heeresgruppe B which was deficient in just about everything needed to produce success.

This had not always been the case, of course. The original Seventh Armee commanded by General Friedrich Dollmann had been formed on August 25 1939, but only played a secondary role in the invasion of France in 1940, forming part of Feldmarschall

SEVENTH ARMEE RESERVE

501 schwere Panzerjäger Abteilung (Festungs)
(This was a static battalion with emplaced weapons –
number and calibre of weapons unknown)

657 & 668 Panzerjäger Abteilungen (mot.Z)
(Each 3 x batterien, each batterie 6 x 7.5cm PaK 40)

406 & 408 Volks-Artillerie Korps
(Each) Stabs Kompanie & Beobachtungs (observation)
Kompanie
I Bataillon
1-3 Batterien (each 6 x 7.5cm FK 40)
II Bataillon
4-5 Batterien (each 6 x 10cm K 18)
III Bataillon
6-8 Batterien (each 6 x 10.5cm leFH 18/40)
IV Bataillon
9-10 Batterien (each 6 x 15.2cm KH 433[r])
V Bataillon
11-12 Batterien (each 6 x 12.2cm sFH 396[r])

8 & 18 Volks-Werfer Brigaden
(Each) Stabs Kompanie, Nachrichten Kompanie &
Park Kompanie
1 Regiment
Stabs Kompanie
I Abteilung
1-3 Batterien (each 6 x 15cm WGr 41)
II Abteilung
4-6 Batterien (each 6 x 15cm WGr 41)
III Abteilung
7-9 Batterien (each 6 x 21cm WGr 42)
2 Regiment
Stabs Kompanie
I & II Abteilungen (as I/ and II/1)
III Abteilung
7-9 Batterien (each 6 x 30cm WkrS 42)

660 schwere Artillerie Batterie
(6 x 15cm sIG 33)

1092, 1093, 1124 & 1125 schwere Haubitze-Artillerie Batterien
(Each 6 x 15cm sFH 18)

1029, 1039 & 1122 schwere Mörser Batterien
(Each 6 x 21cm Mörser 18 or 38)

15 Flak Regiment
(14 x schwere Flak Batterien, each 4 x 8.8cm Flak 18/36, and
12 x leichte/mittlerer Flak Batterien, each 8 x 2cm Flak
30/38 or 3.7cm Flak 18/36)

44 Festungs-Maschinengewehr Bataillon
(Composition unknown; fortress battalion)

XIII/999 Festungs-Infanterie Bataillon
(Composition unknown; penal battalion)

47 Pionier Brigade (mot) (2 x bataillonen)
(Each bataillon) Stabs Kompanie (5 x leMG 42)
1, 2 & 3 Kompanien (each 2 x 8cm GrW 34,
6 x Flammenwerfer, 2 x sMG 42 & 18 x leMG 42)

677 Bau-pionier Bataillon
Stabs Zug
1, 2 & 3 Kompanien (each 6 x leMG 42)
4 Kompanie (2 x leMG 42)

961, 964, 965 & 966 Brückenkollonen (B)
(Each 2 x abteilungen, each abteilung 4 x
kompanien, 4 x pontoon bridge)

974 Brückenkollone (J)
(2 x abteilungen, each abteilung 4 x kompanien,   4 x
girder-bridge)

Wilhelm von Leeb's Heeresgruppe C facing the Maginot Line. It was then assigned the key role in defending the Normandy and Brittany coast for, after the Luftwaffe's defeat in the Battle of Britain and the entry of the United States into the war in 1941, an Allied invasion of France sooner or later was a foregone conclusion. After Dollmann committed suicide on June 30 1944, while his army reeled backwards, SS-Obergruppenführer Paul Hausser took over until its virtual destruction in the Falaise pocket. Erich Brandenberger assumed command on September 3 but was not briefed on his army's intended role until summoned, with Fifth and Sixth Panzer Armee COs Hasso von Manteuffel and 'Sepp' Dietrich, to Model's briefing at Fichtenhain on October 27.

Brandenberger, like Manteuffel and unlike Dietrich or Model, was a product of the old Prussian officer caste. According to Model, the diehard Nazi, he was 'a typical product of the General Staff' with 'the features

The sound of aircraft engines usually spelt trouble for the men of Seventh Armee because the Luftwaffe was conspicuous only by its absence. (Bundesarchiv)

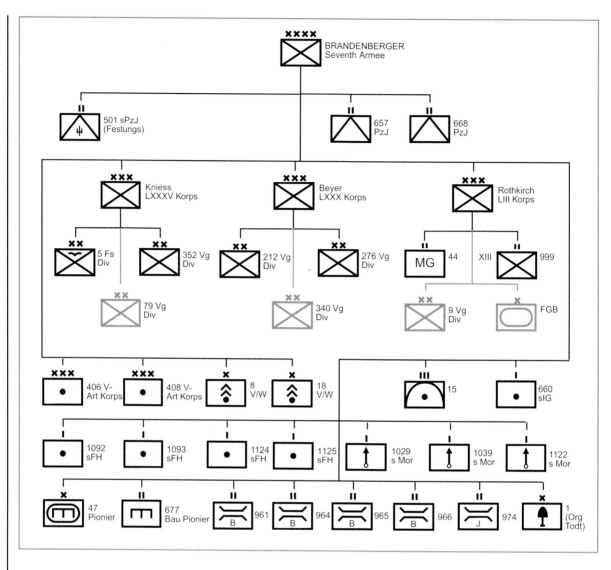

of a scientist'. In contrast, Manteuffel held him in quiet regard since Brandenberger had commanded 8 Panzer Division with skill and determination during the drive on Leningrad in 1941 and the subsequent battles in the central sector of the Russian front during 1942–43. After the battle of Kursk, Brandenberger took over XXIX Korps until he was recalled to the west to assume command of the reconstituted Seventh Armee for operation 'Herbstnebel'.

Compared to Fifth and Sixth Panzer Armees, Seventh Armee was indeed weak, even as it was originally to have been constituted. To give it some extra weight, it was intended that it should have three Volks-Artillerie Korps, instead of which it ended up with only two. Then, because it was severely deficient in armour, it was assigned 25 Panzergrenadier Division with its 5 Panzer Abteilung (rebuilt from the disbanded independent 107 Panzer Brigade) which had 33 Panthers and 11 Jagdpanzer IV/70s. This division could have been decisive in halting Patton's 4th Armored's drive to relieve Bastogne, but instead it was wasted by handing it over to Heeresgruppe G as a mobile reserve for operation 'Nordwind'. The belated transfer of the Führer Grenadier Brigade, with its pot-pourri of AFVs, from OKW reserve to Seventh Armee on December 22 was very much second best.

As a result, Seventh Armee began the campaign with just four infantry divisions: 5 Fallschirm and 352 Volksgrenadier in Baptist Kniess' LXXXV Korps on the right and 212 and 276 Volksgrenadier Divisions in Franz Beyer's LXXX Korps on the left. LIII Korps at this stage, on the far left, was a corps in name only. The only armoured support in the whole of Seventh Armee, apart from the handful of vehicles in the Panzerjäger Abteilungen, was 11 Sturmgeschutz Brigade attached to 5 Fallschirm Division. That this performed as well as it did in delaying Patton's 4th Armored Division only goes to show what the presence of either 25 Panzergrenadier Division or the Führer Grenadier Brigade at the outset of the offensive might have achieved.

Looking at the other figures, Dietrich's Sixth Panzer Armee – the 'figurehead' formation with its four SS-Panzer divisions – had three Volks-Artillerie Korps totalling 685 barrels, 180 of them over 15cm calibre; Brandenberger had two corps with 381 barrels, only 76 of which were over 15cm. Dietrich had three Volks-Werfer Brigaden totalling 340 Nebelwerfers, whereas Brandenberger only had two with 248 rocket launchers. Dietrich had five batteries of heavy mortars and siege artillery – Brandenberger just one. Dietrich had the whole of 2 Flak Division for anti-aircraft support; Brandenberger just had 15 Flak Regiment. Even worse, considering that the river Sauer – always fast-running – was swollen by the rain and snow, Brandenberger's army only had two battalions of combat engineers, one of construction engineers, one of bridge-building engineers and five bridging columns, compared to Dietrich's six engineer battalions and nine bridging columns. Moreover, Brandenberger's obvious bridging sites were well zeroed in by American artillery. This explains Model's order that 'the destruction of the enemy artillery units'

The little town of Wiltz was headquarters of the U.S. 28th Infantry Division until its capture on December 19 and then became the forward HQ for Seventh Armee's LIII Korps. (U.S. Army)

was vital – but without bridges, Brandenberger could not give his infantry any heavy close support weapons to help. The requested 'intensive destruction and minelaying', as well as anti-tank measures, were similarly all but impossible. Brandenberger's chief of staff, Oberst Rudolph Gersdoff, dutifully lodged a formal complaint which Model, of course, ignored.

Whatever his many faults, though, Model had not earned himself the nickname 'Führer's Fireman' on the Russian front for nothing, as his prompt reactions at Arnhem earlier in 1944 had also proved. Once it became clear that Dietrich's Sixth Panzer Armee blitzkrieg was faltering and that Manteuffel's Fifth was making significantly better progress, Model turned his enterprising mind to the several ways in which he could sustain the momentum of the offensive. To this end, on December 22, he released several divisions and brigades from reserve. Brandenberger was at last to receive some armour in the shape of the elite Führer Grenadier Brigade, and two fresh infantry divisions, 9 and 79 Volksgrenadier.

Because the obstinate defence of Bastogne had already become a deeply irritating thorn on Fifth Panzer Armee's left flank, Model assigned 9 Volksgrenadier Division and the Führer Grenadier Brigade to Seventh Armee's right. Instead of placing them under command of Kniess' LXXXV Korps, however, he moved the so far unemployed LIII Korps staff from their comfortable billets in Trier and gave them command of these two new formations plus 5 Fallschirm Division – which by then was out on a limb with its own southern flank unprotected because

Given Seventh Armee's weaknesses in armour and anti-tank artillery, it was fortunate that the Volksgrenadiers had a high allocation of Panzerfausts, with 54 in each regiment's 14 Kompanie alone – enough to take out an entire American tank battalion! Having a much greater punch than the bazooka, the Panzerfaust (and Panzerschreck) were the two most effective hand-held anti-tank weapons of the war.
(U.S. Signal Corps)

of the relative lethargy of 352 Volksgrenadier Division. Similarly, Model plugged the gap between 5 Fallschirm Division and the rest of Seventh Armee by giving 79 Volksgrenadier Division to Kniess, although tactically it actually acted as though part of LIII Korps and was eventually absorbed by it.

Brandenberger had no control over these dispositions, and whether he agreed with them or not, he had to live with them. At fifty years of age, he was well accustomed to taking orders. What he could not have foreseen was Model's visit to his headquarters on February 20 1945. The Field Marshal gave him a public rebuke for his 'failure' and dismissed him, putting General der Infanterie Hans Felber from Fifteenth Armee in his place. However unfair, this may have actually saved Brandenberger's life because, shortly after he departed, Allied aircraft bombed his HQ and injured Felber. Whether Brandenberger had a quiet smile to himself when Model later committed suicide is unknown …

That Seventh Armee failed to achieve all of its objectives is no surprise. That it succeeded in some is a tribute not just to Erich Brandenberger but to all the officers and men he commanded – many of them barely trained, let alone combat veterans. What Seventh Armee achieved is largely skirted over in histories of 'the Bulge' – but not forgotten by the men of George Patton's III and XII Corps!

Almost the end of the road for Seventh Armee. A StuG III (note early style mantlet) from 5 Kompanie of I/101 Panzer Regiment 'FGB' is examined closely by curious GIs outside Heiderscheid. Originally designed as assault guns for the infantry support role, the Sturmgeschütze were increasingly used as tank destroyers as the war progressed.
(U.S. Army)

SEVENTH ARMEE

LXXXV KORPS

General der Infanterie Baptist Kniess' LXXXV Korps – the only one in Seventh Armee with any armoured 'muscle' at all, and that was pathetically inadequate – was given the most ambitious and, needless to say, unattainable mission. Hitler even had his sights set on the Korps penetrating west of Luxembourg City to Arlon, just over the Belgian frontier, where Patton established his III Corps' headquarters! Fortunately, Model, with Jodl's support, was able to convince the Führer that this really was impossible, but the task assigned to Kniess was still too much for his limited manpower and resources. This, however, was nothing new to Kniess.

First formed in 1940, LXXXV Korps was only peripherally involved in 'Fall Gelb' and after the defeat of France was assigned occupation duties. At the end of 1942, following the Allied landings in French northwest Africa, the Korps moved into the formerly unoccupied Vichy sector and took up station on the Mediterranean coast, commanded by Generaloberst Friedrich Wiese. When the latter was promoted to

> **LXXXV KORPS**
> General der Infanterie Baptist Kneiss
> Stab
>
> ---
>
> 5 Fallschirm Division (Heilmann)
> (to LIII Korps December 22)
> 79 Volksgrenadier Division (Weber)
> (from Heeresgruppe B Reserve December 22)
> 352 Volksgrenadier Division (Schmidt)
> 11 Fallschirm-Sturmgeschutz Brigade (Hollunder)
> 406 Volks-Artillerie Korps
> 18 Volks-Werfer Brigade

General der Infanterie on October 1, 1943, he took over command of Nineteenth Armee and Baptist Kniess was appointed to replace him as CO of LXXXV Korps.

Kniess himself had been on the staff of I Korps during the invasion of France in 1940 and Russia in 1941, and was not given his first independent field

Although LXXXV Korps had the whole of 406 Volks-Artillerie Korps attached from Armee Reserve, ammunition shortages severely curtailed its effectiveness in supporting either the attack or the later defence. Here, grenadiers carry shells still packed in their wicker containers up to a gun battery.
(Suddeutscher)

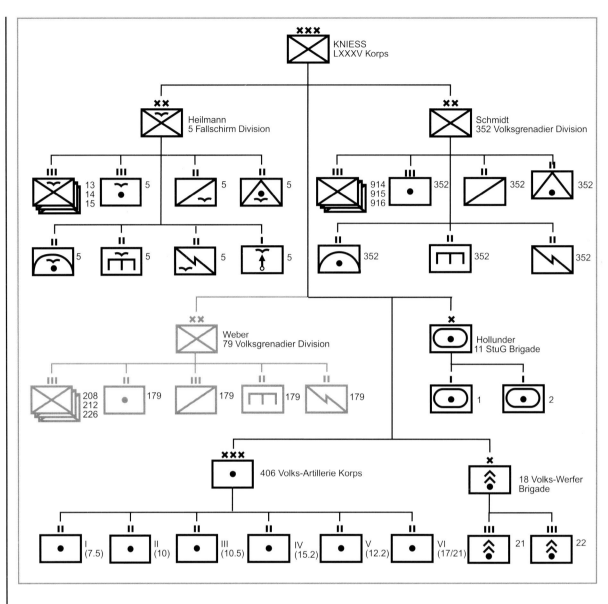

command until 1942 when, with the rank of Generalleutnant, he took over 26 Infanterie Division from Walter Weiss. With his own promotion to General der

LXXXV KORPS RESERVE

11 Fallschirm-Sturmgeschutz Brigade
(attached to 5 Fallschirm Division) (c. 350 men)
(Two kompanien, each c.10 x Stug III according to the CO)

406 Volks-Artillerie Korps (from Armee Reserve)
(As Armee Reserve data)

18 Volks-Werfer Brigade (from Armee Reserve)
21 & 22 Volks-Werfer Regimenter
(As Armee Reserve data)

Infanterie next year, Kniess joined LXXXV Korps on the right, or western, flank of Nineteenth Armee with his headquarters in Marseilles. When the Allies landed on the Riviera in August 1944, the Korps retreated prudently alongside the rest of Nineteenth Armee up the Rhône valley and was heavily engaged in the autumn battles against the U.S. Seventh Army in Lorraine and Alsace. Then, with the bulk of Nineteenth Armee trapped in the Colmar pocket west of the Rhein, Kniess and his staff were re-assigned to Seventh Armee on December 2, and the reconstituted LXXXV Korps took up station on its northern flank for operation 'Herbstnebel'.

Kniess' task was complicated by the fact that, unlike LXXX Korps to his south, his men had first to assault over the river Our around Vianden before even reaching the Sûre. This put them in no worse a situation than the Fifth Panzer Armee forces to their north (specifically, General Heinrich von Lüttwitz's XLVII Panzer Korps), who had to cross the Our and the Clerf as well. But, as we have seen, Seventh Armee was deficient in both engineers and bridging equipment, on top of which the American artillery had all their likely bridging sites zeroed in.

On the plus side of the equation, although he did not know it, all that Kniess' two divisions had immediately facing them was a single regiment, the 109th, of the U.S. 28th Infantry Division which was severely understrength and weary after its long ordeal in the Hürtgen Forest earlier in the winter. Even though Brandenberger's orders to his Korps commanders restricted them to putting only two of each division's three regiments into the initial assault, Kniess' Korps enjoyed a numerical superiority approaching four to one in the front line, with plenty in reserve. Statistically, this is the right ratio to assure victory in an attack against prepared positions, unless there are unforeseen circumstances; and up until the intervention of Patton's III Corps (Major-General John Millikin) from the south, the Korps' attack went remarkably smoothly, overall, although Brandenberger was dissatisfied and so, at the end of the day, was Model.

On the Korps' right flank it was the task of Generalmajor Ludwig Heilmann's 5 Fallschirm Division to cross the Our at Vianden and Stolzembourg with its assault companies while a bridge was built at Roth for the self-propelled guns of the attached 11 StuG Brigade. Work on the bridge was hampered by the fact that there was an enormous bomb crater on the eastern bank of the river which had to be filled in first, and by incessant and accurate American artillery fire. Nevertheless, the bridge was operable by nightfall on the second day of the attack. Even before this, though, the StuG brigade commander, Oberst Hollunder, had managed to get a few of his vehicles across the Our over the top of a weir near Vianden.

Meanwhile, on the division's right flank, 14 Fallschirm Regiment – whose attack fell at the junction of the U.S. 109th and 110th Infantry Regiments – found its task simplified because the 110th was already more than busy coping with von Lüttwitz's XLVII Panzer Korps. The paras found the going relatively unopposed after crossing the Our at Stolzembourg but ran into stiff resistance from Company I of III/110th at Weiler and Hoscheid, which was not overcome until late on the 17th. The regiment, betraying the lack of discipline which the division's commander had lamented, then got sucked into XLVII Panzer Korps' attack at Wiltz, totally against Heilmann's orders.

On the division's left, 15 Fallschirm Regiment's assault companies crossed the Our at Vianden and, finding a gap between Companies E and F of the U.S. 109th Regiment at Führen (Fouren) and on the Stolzembourg heights, pushed unopposed through Walsdorf towards Bourscheid. Ignoring the temptation to get involved in the battle for Wiltz, the regiment's commander, Oberstleutnant Kurt Gröschke, pushed his men on westward across the Clerf, following the north bank of the Sûre to reach Martelange on December 21. The regiment thus became the only unit involved in operation 'Herbstnebel' to accomplish its prime directive, because Martelange blocks the main road from Luxembourg City and Arlon to Bastogne,

Ettelbruck lies at the confluence of the rivers Alzette and Wark just west of where they converge with the Sûre, and after its capture by 352 Volksgrenadier Division formed the southern pivot point for LXXXV Korps.
(U.S. Signal Corps)

Lacking any really effective armoured support, the men of LXXXV Korps were quick to press any captured American tanks into their own service. The Balkenkreuz can faintly be seen on the lower front hull of this M4, now turretless, from the 707th Tank Battalion. It had been captured in Wiltz by men of 14 Fallschirm Regiment. (U.S. Signal Corps)

and this was where – quite rightly – Model and Brandenberger expected Patton's Third Army's main initial riposte to fall.

On the Fallschirmjägers' own left flank, Oberst Erich Schmidt's 352 Volksgrenadier Division assaulted across the Our under cover of a heavy barrage from the Korps' artillery. The first waves of grenadiers were camouflaged by the early morning fog which had rolled in, and the American outposts of Company I, III/109th, were rapidly overrun or bypassed, while engineers started work on a bridge for the supporting horse-drawn artillery at Gentingen. Even though word of the attack did not reach Lieutenant-Colonel James Rudder's command post in Ettelbruck until 0900 hrs, his artillery was quickly in action to delay the bridge's construction, as U.S. guns were everywhere else down Seventh Armee's front.

On 352 Volksgrenadier Division's right flank, paralleling 15 Fallschirm Regiment, Schmidt's 915 Grenadier Regiment cut off the company of GIs in Führen which the paras had bypassed and headed west through Longsdorf and Tandel, although the latter village had to be recaptured after a spirited counter-attack. On the division's left, 916 Grenadier Regiment was pinned down by artillery fire outside Hösdorf. By the following day, however, the bridge at Gentingen had also been completed and Schmidt pushed his reserve 914 Grenadier Regiment forward in between the leading two. This produced the desired result. Führen fell and, as the grenadiers advanced through Bettendorff (where, however, American engineers had blown the bridge over the river Wark), Colonel Rudder pulled the remnants of II and III/109th back to Diekirch. The little town lacked any natural defensive features and, although the GIs held out against several waves of grenadiers on the 19th, Rudder evacuated Diekirch

during the night, pulling the two battalions back to supporting positions behind the rivers Wark, Sûre and Alzette either side of the 1st Battalion in Ettelbruck.

352 Volksgrenadier Division, minus its commander who had been badly wounded while personally leading an assault at Diekirch, pursued the Americans and attacked either side of Ettelbruck on the 20th, forcing Colonel Rudder to pull his regiment still further back towards the southwest and the tanks of 9th Armored Division's Combat Command A, establishing a new defensive line around Vichten. On the 21st the grenadiers raced into the vacuum thus created to capture Merzig and Grosbous, and 915 Grenadier Regiment got as far west as Pratz. This, however, was the high tide mark of the Korps' advance and on the 22nd 5 Fallschirm Division passed to LIII Korps. To replace it, Kniess got the newly arrived 79 Volksgrenadier Division but from this point on, apart from localised counter-attacks against Patton's advancing 26th and 80th Infantry Divisions, the rest of the Korps' battle was purely defensive.

After 5 Fallschirm and 352 Volksgrenadier Divisions crossed the river Our, forcing the U.S. 109th Regiment to fall steadily back to the southwest and separating it from its parent 28th Infantry Division, the two divisions of LXXXV Korps found themselves increasingly separated as well by the natural barrier of the river Sûre. By December 22 they were, in effect, fighting totally separate battles and it was as much to plug the dangerous vacuum in between them as to reinforce them that Model released 9 and 79 Volksgrenadier Divisions and the Führer Grenadier Brigade from reserve. Then, to shorten the over-extended Korps' front, he brought the LIII Korps staff up from Trier to take over command of Seventh Armee's northern flank.

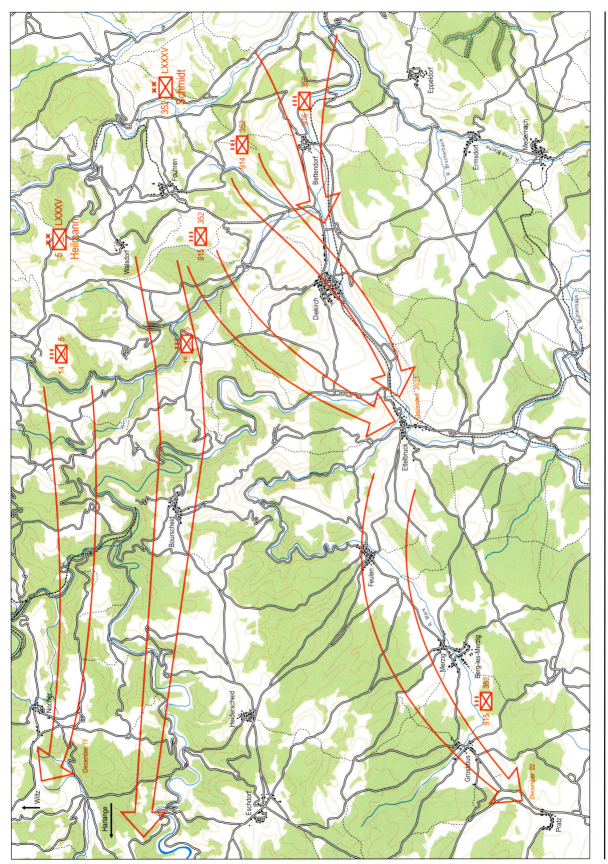

5 Fallschirm Division

Generalmajor 'König Ludwig' Heilmann's 5 Fallschirm Division on Seventh Armee's right flank was given one of the most difficult tasks in the whole of operation 'Herbstnebel' and, although its performance was erratic, it was the sole division out of all three armies to achieve all of its

Seen here with the rank of Major while fighting with 3 Fallschirm Regiment, 1 Fallschirm Division, in Russia in 1942, Ludwig Heilmann took over command of the regiment as Oberst when it was transferred to Italy, and conducted a brilliant defence at Cassino. (Bundesarchiv)

assigned objectives. This was all the more remarkable under the circumstances because it was plagued by internal problems. Heilmann, nicknamed 'the King' by his men, was a hero of the battles for Crete and Cassino and even held the same decoration as the CO of Ob West, Feldmarschall Gerd von Rundstedt: the Knight's Cross with Oakleaves and Swords.

However, because he had transferred from the Heer to the Luftwaffe after the 1939–40 campaigns (rising from company commander in 21 Infanterie Regiment to battalion commander in 3 Fallschirm Regiment in the process), Heilmann was intensely disliked by Kurt Student, the 'founding father' of the Fallschirmjäger. Perhaps it was also because the commander of Tenth Armee in Italy, General Heinrich von Vietinghoff, said that 'No troops but [Heilmann's] could have held Cassino.' The dislike was reciprocated, but when Heilmann was appointed CO of 5 Fallschirm Division in the autumn of 1944 (at Hitler's insistence), he found his staff packed with unco-operative Student protégés. On top of this, the division's personnel were, bluntly, both untrained and often undisciplined, but Heilmann's complaints to Model about their fitness fell on deaf ears.

The original 5 Fallschirm Division commanded by Generalmajor Gustav Wilke had been formed at

---

5 FALLSCHIRM DIVISION
Generalmajor Ludwig Heilmann
Stabs Kompanie

---

13 Fallschirm Regiment
14 Fallschirm Regiment
15 Fallschirm Regiment (Gröschke)
5 Fallschirm-Artillerie Regiment
5 Fallschirm-Aufklärungs Abteilung
5 Fallschirm-Panzerjäger Abteilung
5 Fallschirm-Flak Abteilung
5 Fallschirm-Pionier Bataillon
5 Fallschirm-Nachrichten Abteilung
5 Fallschirm schwere Mörser Batterie
5 Fallschirm Nachschub Truppe
5 Fallschirm Werkstatt Truppe
5 Fallschirm Verwaltungs Truppe
5 Fallschirm Sanitäts Truppe
11 Falschirm-Sturmgeschutz Brigade (Hollunder)
 (attached from Korps Reserve)

Reims in March 1943 from XI Flieger Korps' Lehr Bataillon and was stationed near Rennes in June 1944. It was considered an elite formation and was rushed from Brittany to Normandy, where it fought well but, after Falaise, was reported by the then commander of Seventh Armee, SS-Obergruppenführer Paul Hausser, as 'practically destroyed'. Its remnants were absorbed by 275 Infanterie Division and Wilke took over a re-formed 2 Fallschirm Division after the fall of Brest.

A new 5 Fallschirm division was also formed in Holland from Luftwaffe ground personnel and, although it was virtually at full strength for 'Herbstnebel' with nearly 16,000 men, it was packed with battle-inexperienced misfits who enjoyed being called 'paras' but had none of their training or esprit de corps. This resulted in their overlapping with, and sometimes getting in the way of, Fifth Panzer Armee's left flank units (Panzer Lehr and 26 Volksgrenadier Divisions).

The division assembled near Bitburg early in December and crossed the river Our at Stolzembourg on the 16th while engineers constructed a bridge at Roth for the twenty assault guns in Oberstleutnant

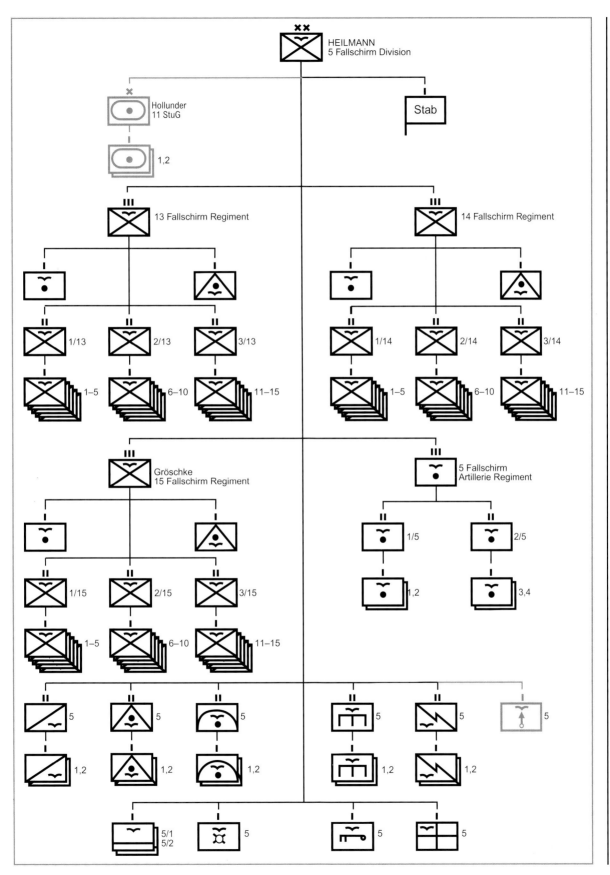

HEILMANN
5 Fallschirm Division

Hollunder
11 StuG

1,2

Stab

13 Fallschirm Regiment

14 Fallschirm Regiment

1/13

2/13

3/13

1–5

6–10

11–15

1/14

2/14

3/14

1–5

6–10

11–15

Gröschke
15 Fallschirm Regiment

5 Fallschirm
Artillerie Regiment

1/15

2/15

3/15

1–5

6–10

11–15

1/5

2/5

1,2

3,4

5

5

5

5

5

5

1,2

1,2

1,2

1,2

1,2

5/1
5/2

5

5

5

During their unauthorised foray into Wiltz, the men of 14 Fallschirm Regiment captured this M4 from the 707th Tank Battalion, painted prominent Balkan crosses on it and left it guarding the sharp road bend around the Hôtel des Ardennes in Esch-sur-Sûre, where it remained to be knocked out during the Allied counter-attack. Although rebuilt, the hotel still stands.
(U.S. Army)

Hollunder's attached 11 Sturmgeschutz Brigade. The men reached Walsdorf unopposed, took Hoscheid after a fierce battle and by the 18th were across the Clerf. Now, while 14 Fallschirm Regiment became involved, against orders, in the unnecessary battle for Wiltz on the 19th, 15 Fallschirm Regiment pressed on to its principal objective, Martelange, which it reached on the 21st.

The same day, 14 Fallschirm Regiment on its right helped in the capture of Sibret, sealing Bastogne off from the outside world. This completed the division's initial mission of establishing a southern shoulder for Fifth Panzer Armee's drive to the Meuse, but then Patton's Third Army counter-attacked, which was the beginning of the end for the whole campaign and not just 5 Fallschirm Division.

On December 22, the division passed to General Friedrich von Rothkirch's LIII Korps whose staff had been moved from the southern flank of Seventh Armee to the northern. It was joined by the freshly committed Führer Grenadier Brigade released from OKW reserve which entered the battle on the division's left, and later by 276 Volksgrenadier Division from LXXX Korps.

Meanwhile, at Martelange, where the bridge over the Sûre had been destroyed, 15 Fallschirm Regiment exchanged shots with CCA of 4th Armored Division before retiring, while 14 Fallschirm Regiment also delayed CCB at Burnon before falling back on Chaumont during the night. Here, on the 23rd, Heilmann counter-attacked with a company of Hollunder's StuGs and forced the Americans to retire, while 15 Fallschirm Regiment held CCA up at Warnach until Christmas Day. On their right, however, tanks from 4th Armored's CCR broke through the 39th Regiment of 26 Volksgrenadier Division at Assenois to reach Bastogne on Boxing Day.

The Fallschirmjäger continued to resist against increasing pressure from the U.S. III Corps over the next few days, and 14 Fallschirm Regiment was attached to XXXIX Panzer Korps for the counter-attack around Lutrebois on December 30. Fighting on the Korps' left flank, the regiment seized Villers-la-Bonne-Eau and took the surrender of two companies from the 35th Infantry Division, then repulsed counter-attacks. The operation overall, however, was a failure and the Americans pressed on with expanding the Bastogne corridor, beginning their own strategic counter-offensive on January 3.

Heilmann's division continued to resist throughout January, only grudgingly conceding ground, but by February it had been reduced to the size of a kampfgruppe. Defeated by Patton's forces at Prüm, the survivors were re-allocated to Fifteenth Armee and a month later, trapped with their backs to the Rhein, the majority surrendered, their commander amongst them. Only a few stragglers escaped east to meet their own fate in the Ruhr pocket.

79 Volksgrenadier Division

O f all the ill-equipped and understrength units involved in Operation 'Herbstnebel', Oberst Alois Weber's 79 Volksgrenadier Division appeared on paper to be about the worst, yet the 'formidable' fighting quality of its infantrymen was highly praised after the battle by U.S. Intelligence. There was, in truth, nothing else to applaud, because the division had no anti-tank or anti-aircraft guns, nor any StuGs in December 1944, and what vehicles it did possess were makeshift or battle weary.

Moreover, most of its personnel had been combed out from headquarters clerks and others with little or no combat training or experience. This did not inspire confidence in their CO, Alois Weber, a veteran of the Russian front who had commanded the 61st Regiment in 7 Infanterie Division at Kursk and in August 1944 had briefly been the acting divisional commander.

His new 79 Volksgrenadier Division was in Heeresgruppe B reserve at the beginning of the battle but Model released it to Brandenberger on December 22. With the transfer of 5 Fallschirm Division to LIII Korps on the same date, Brandenberger assigned the 79th to LXXXV Korps, placing it in the line on the right of 352 Volksgrenadier Division where it was soon in action against Major-General Horace McBride's 80th Infantry Division.

The 79th had already had a long war by this stage, most of it fought in Russia. Raised predominantly from Rheinlanders in the summer of 1939 with its home station at Koblenz, it saw brief action against the French on the Saar front in 1940 and was then assigned to Heeresgruppe Süd for the invasion of Russia in June 1941. After fighting its way across the Ukraine to the river Dniepr, it took part in the great battle of encirclement around Kiev before falling on to the defensive during the Soviet winter counter-offensive. In 1942 the division fought at Kharkov and Voronezh as well as in the subsequent encirclement battles at Izyum and Kalack, but was then unfortunate enough to be trapped itself in Stalingrad, where most of its men went into Russian captivity, including their commander, Generalleutnant Alexander von Daniels.

A second 79 Infanterie Division was promptly raised and again sent to the south of Russia. During the summer of 1943 it fought in the Kuban bridgehead before being evacuated back to the Ukraine via the Crimea. By

79 VOLKSGRENADIER DIVISION

Oberst Alois Weber

Stabs Kompanie

208 Volksgrenadier Regiment
212 Volksgrenadier Regiment
226 Volksgrenadier Regiment
179 Volks-Artillerie Regiment
179 Pionier Bataillon
79 Nachrichten Abteilung
1179 Nachschub Truppe
1179 Werkstatt Truppe
1179 Verwaltungs Truppe
1179 Sanitäts Truppe

1944, as part of Generalleutnant Friedrich Mieth's IV Korps in the reconstituted Sixth Armee, it was back in Romania. When Romania capitulated on August 23, the Korps was cut off and had to try to fight its way out but was virtually annihilated on the river Berlad; Mieth was killed and Generalleutnant Friedrich Weinknecht became the second of 79 Infanterie Division's COs to be captured. In fact, only one man escaped the débâcle to rejoin German lines twelve days after the battle.

A third 79th was raised in Poland as a Volksgrenadier Division in October, absorbing 586 Volksgrenadier Division, which had started forming the previous month. Now commanded by Alois Weber, it was moved west in December but was still only at about half strength at the beginning of 'Herbstnebel' and had very little field artillery since most of it was still entangled in the traffic jams miles to the east which were so delaying all reinforcements to the front. Fortuitously, therefore, Weber's men stumbled on a battalion belonging to 5 Fallschirm Division which had been left behind when all its towing vehicles broke down. 79 Volksgrenadier Division, of course, had horses to perform the same task and the guns were quickly pressed into service to support a counter-attack from Eschdorf toward Heiderscheid on Christmas Eve.

The American battalion in Heiderscheid had repulsed one assault by the Führer Grenadier Brigade the previous day and now Weber launched a dawn attack by two of his infantry battalions supported by a mixture of FGB armoured fighting vehicles. It almost succeeded after a fierce hand-to-hand battle, but the Americans called down an intense artillery barrage and, caught in the open, Weber's grenadiers had no option but to retire after taking heavy casualties. Over the next couple of days they got their revenge though. Weber established his command post in Bourscheid and his grenadiers relentlessly repelled three assaults around Welscheid by the 317th Regiment, 80th Infantry Division, causing such heavy casualties that the Americans called the attack off.

Except in the area to the immediate southeast of Bastogne, most of the exhausted men on both sides of the Seventh Armee front now had a brief respite until the main Allied counter-offensive began on January 3, with the 80th Infantry Division again assaulting 79 Volksgrenadier Division on the 5th. Three days later Model authorised the start of a general

withdrawal and 79 Volksgrenadier Division began a slow retreat northeast.

By the end of the month almost all the territory captured during 'Herbstnebel' had been lost again apart from a small bridgehead west of Dasburg and Vianden – the 'Vianden pocket'. 79 Volksgrenadier Division, now with LIII Korps, had by this time been reduced to fewer than 4,000 men but held the pocket open in the face of intensive Allied air raids in order to allow as many men as possible from Fifth and Seventh Armees to get back across the river Our.

Under its final commander, Oberst Kurt Hummel, 79 Volksgrenadier Division absorbed the remnants of 276 Volksgrenadier Division from LIII Korps and was then heavily engaged at Bitburg in February. The following month it was dissolved, with the survivors being parcelled out amongst other Seventh Armee formations.

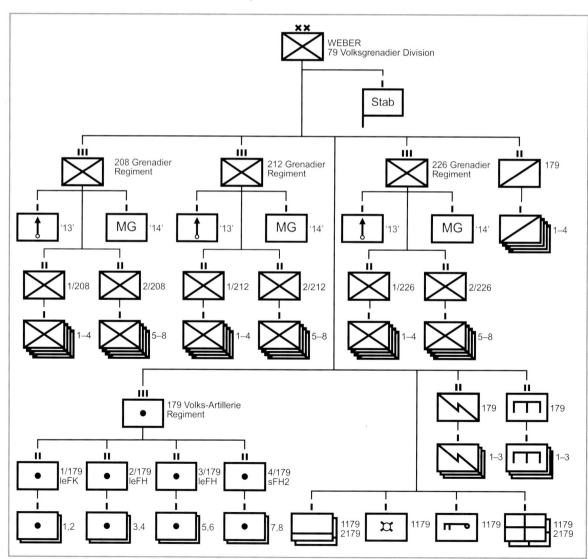

352 Volksgrenadier Division

Generalmajor Erich Schmidt's 352 Volks-grenadier Division was already in position behind the river Sûre east of Ettelbruck before the preparations for 'Herbstnebel' were implemented, so his men knew the terrain well. All they had to do during the couple of nights preceding the assault was reshuffle their battalions a little in order to make room for the 15th Regiment of 5 Fallschirm Division to move in on their right, and permit 276 Volksgrenadier Division from LXXX Korps to occupy the river line to their left. Their next task proved more difficult. The intention was, after crossing the Our at Gentingen, to secure the wooded heights overlooking the road which winds from Arlon in the west, through Bissen to Ettelbruck, thus protecting the eastern extremity of 5 Fallschirm Division's left flank. Facing them was Lieutenant-Colonel James Rudder's 109th Regiment of the U.S. 28th Infantry Division, and here we encounter one of the war's many strange coincidences. Before that, it is necessary to backtrack.

The 352nd was a mid-war formation raised at Hannover in November 1943 from raw recruits around a nucleus of veterans from 268 Infanterie Division, which had been virtually destroyed at Kursk in July, and 321 Infanterie Division, which had also met its demise on the Russian front in October the same year. During training, it was commanded by Generalmajor Eberhard Schuckmann but when posted to Normandy in January 1944 its CO was Generalleutnant Dietrich Kraiss.

On the Allied side, Montgomery's head of intelligence, Brigadier Bill Williams, alerted Omar Bradley – then commanding the U.S. First Army – to the arrival of Kraiss' fresh 352 Infanterie Division in his 'Omaha' sector of the D-Day beaches, but the warning passed unheeded. Even if the information had been relayed, it is difficult to see what the commander of the 1st Infantry Division, Major-General Clarence Huebner, could have done about it. He and his men knew they were in for a tough fight and that they had to win their way off the beaches, so what did it matter who exactly their opponents were? The man who did fail Huebner was his Corps commander, Leonard Gerow, who had refused the British offer of some of 79th Armoured Division's specialised 'Funnies' to aid the assault. His infantry and combat engineers, he

---

352 VOLKSGRENADIER DIVISION
Oberst (later Generalmajor) Erich Schmidt
Stabs Kompanie

---

914 Volksgrenadier Regiment
915 Volksgrenadier Regiment
916 Volksgrenadier Regiment
352 Füsilier Kompanie
352 Volks-Artillerie Regiment
352 Aufklärungs Abteilung
352 Panzerjäger Abteilung (mot)
352 Flak Abteilung (?)
352 Pionier Bataillon
352 Nachrichten Abteilung
1352 Nachschub Truppe
1352 Werkstatt Truppe
1352 Verwaltungs Truppe
1352 Sanitäts Truppe

---

was certain, could carry the day. In fact, it was only with reluctance that Gerow had accepted 96 Duplex-Drive Shermans to assist the assault, and the first wave of 32 of these was launched so far offshore that 27 of them were swamped and sank in the six-foot waves, drowning their crews.

To some extent, Gerow's overconfidence could be justified because Kraiss actually had only a single rifle regiment on the 'Omaha' front between Pointe de la Percée in the west and Porte-en-Bessin in the east, the 916th. The 914th on its left was thinly spread almost as far west as Carentan, where the paras of Freiherr von der Heydte's 6 Fallschirm Regiment took over, while the 915th was in reserve outside Bayeux. On the division's right, the defence of the Anglo-Canadian 'Gold', 'Juno' and 'Sword' beaches was entrusted to Generalleutnant Wilhelm Richter's 716 Infanterie Division's sole two regiments, the 726th and 736th, backed by Generalleutnant Edgar Feuch-tinger's 21 Panzer Division at Caen.

Kraiss' 916 Regiment was well dug-in with concrete and sandbagged emplacements able to give brutal enfilading machine-gun, mortar and artillery fire along the whole shore line. He was confident that the Allies, if they came, would not be able to get ashore easily. The five-mile (8km) stretch of gently sloping beach

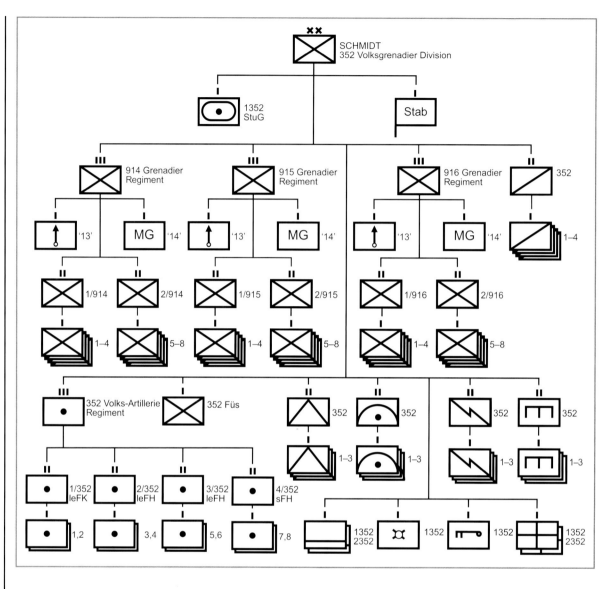

rises to a high tide bank of shingle, behind which is a low sea wall and then the bluffs, bisected by numerous gullies which give access to the inland plateau 150ft (45m) above sea level. The low tide line in 1944 was strewn with steel obstacles designed to rip the bottoms out of landing craft, the feet of the terraced bluffs were protected by minefields, and dense barbed wire entanglements guarded the gullies. Behind these defences, 916 Regiment had a second line of trenches, minefields and gun emplacements.

The U.S. 1st and 29th Infantry Divisions' assault on the morning of June 6 is nowhere more vividly or movingly portrayed than in the film *Saving Private Ryan*. As the landing craft ramps swung down, the cold, wet and seasick men were scythed down by Kraiss' machine-gunners. Many leapt into the sea to avoid the murderous fire and took illusory shelter

behind the angle iron obstacles. Dazed and bewildered, blinded by smoke and flying sand, deafened by explosions and weighted down by their waterlogged equipment, Gerow's men could neither advance nor retreat; death lay in both directions. At the end of an hour it looked as though the invasion had failed, but gradually the paralysis wore off and, singly and in small groups, men ran or crawled to the shelter of the shingle bank or the sea wall.

Combat engineers in the second wave, although hampered by the loss of much of their equipment in the sea, brought up Bangalore torpedoes to blow holes through the minefields and wire, but three hours after the first men waded ashore they were still no closer to achieving any of their objectives. Finally, a company from the 2nd Ranger Battalion managed to claw a precarious hold on top of the bluff at the

The mud in Normandy where 352 Infanterie Division defended 'Omaha' beach was little different from that in the Ardennes, but if there was heavy rain at least there was no snow. (Ullstein)

western, Vierville, end of the beach. Their CO was Lieutenant-Colonel James Rudder.

As more DD Shermans finally got ashore, and a handful of bulldozers began clearing lanes through the obstacles, more groups of men up and down the beach began to emulate the Rangers and one by one the German pillboxes were taken out with grenades, satchel charges and flamethrowers. By nightfall, though, despite the fact that in places the infantry had managed to get as much as a mile inland, 'Omaha' was still far from secure and the guns of 352 Artillerie Regiment continued to pound the beach. Kraiss' Division had inflicted a terrible toll, and if they had had the Panzer backup which Rommel wanted, it is unlikely that a single GI would have got off the beach except as a prisoner.

As it was, the Americans, and the British and Canadians on their left, were slowly able to extend their beachheads, forcing Kraiss' 914th Regiment out of Isigny on June 8 while the 915th similarly had to vacate Bayeux. However, the nature of the countryside now came to 352 Infanterie Division's aid. The dense hedgerows of the bocage prevented the Allies from exploiting their numerical and matériel superiority, and each day's advance was measured in mere yards. Gradually, however, sheer pressure forced the division back as far as St Lô. Possession of this critical road junction was vital to both sides, and to take it the Americans had to use three whole divisions. The battle lasted seven days and cost them over 6,000 casualties, but the 352nd's losses were also high and, after the division finally evacuated the town during the night of July 17/18, it was at barely better than battalion strength and was temporarily absorbed by 2 Panzer Division.

In September the division was reconstituted by renumbering 581 Grenadier Division, which was in the process of being formed at Flensburg. Most of its personnel were Kriegsmarine but it incorporated as a veteran nucleus the survivors from the original formation plus those from 389 Infanterie Division, which had been virtually destroyed at Cherkassy. Training took until mid-November, after which 352 Volksgrenadier Division, now commanded by Generalmajor Erich Schmidt, reassembled at Bitburg prior to taking its place in the line between Vianden and Echternach. It then closed ranks to allow 5 Fallschirm and 276 Volksgrenadier Divisions to move in on its flanks.

The division was at virtually full strength for the new offensive with 13,000 men but had only half a dozen Hetzers in its Panzerjäger Abteilung. Nevertheless, Schmidt considered it to be in pretty good shape and its morale was high. To begin with, as well, it made good progress, capturing Bettendorf, Diekirch and Ettelbruck while Rudder's 109th steadily retired southwest. Half of the heights overlooking the Ettelbruck–Arlon road were secured with 915 Regiment's capture of Pratz on December 22, apart for an enclave of the 109th still dug in around Vichten. Unfortunately, the 352nd's CO had been seriously wounded while personally leading an assault at Diekirch, and command was assumed by a Generalmajor Bazing. Further misfortune lay around the corner.

III Corps of Patton's Third Army had commenced its counter-attack to relieve Bastogne on the same day as the fall of Pratz, and its right-hand 80th Division, after relieving the 109th Regiment at Vichten, pushed north towards Merzig and Ettelbruck. The tail of the 352nd's 915 Regiment was strung out in column along the Ettelbruck–Pratz road and was caught in flank. The Americans sliced through the column, throwing the regiment into total disarray and cutting it off in an enclave around Grosbous and Merzig. Many of its men did eventually make it back to friendly lines, but had to abandon much of their equipment. Similarly, although 914 Regiment managed to occupy Ettelbruck and repulse a number of counter-attacks, it was forced to evacuate the town in the face of a sustained America artillery barrage. This effectively marked the end of the division's offensive operations and, although it continued to resist doggedly, it was as inexorably forced back as it had been after D-Day. By March both 914 and 916 Regiments had been destroyed and the survivors crossed the Rhein to form a kampfgruppe. Finally attached to XIII SS-Korps, the division's last battle was in the defence of Nürnberg in April 1945.

LXXXV KORPS' BATTLES

14 Fallschirm Regiment

Hoscheid/Wiltz/Sibret – December 16–21

All that immediately faced Ludwig Heilmann's leading two regiments when they began crossing the river Our between Stolzembourg and Vianden was a single battalion, the 2nd, of Lieutenant-Colonel James Rudder's 109th Infantry Regiment; and one company of the 110th, both from the U.S. 28th Infantry Division. These two regiments, as with the whole of the rest of the American division, had suffered grievously in the earlier Hürtgen Forest battles and, although they were now back up to almost full strength, their ranks were filled with inexperienced replacements. Heilmann's task should, therefore, have been comparatively easy, but his men encountered exactly the same problems as those faced by Fifth Panzer Armee to their north, with small pockets of resistance causing constant delays to their schedule.

Before dawn on December 16 the engineers of 5 Fallschirm-Pionier Bataillon began ferrying the assault companies of 14 Fallschirm Regiment across the Our. Their instructions were to head as rapidly as possible west to the river Clerf, establish a bridging site at or near Kautenbach, and press on west of Wiltz to establish a blocking line behind the river Sûre south of Bastogne. Their line of advance actually lay at the intersection of the U.S. 109th and 110th Infantry Regiments, and immediately in their path at Weiler was Company I of Major Harold Milton's III/110th, with the divisional command post further west in Wiltz. Heilmann's orders to both his 14th and 15th Regiments called on them to bypass any pockets of resistance in the villages, leaving those to be mopped up later by his reserve 13th Regiment. What was crucial was getting bridges across the Our and Clerf so that Oberst Hollunder's attached 11 StuG Brigade could add its muscle to the attack, and the divisional artillery could be brought forward in support. Unfortunately, due to the lack of discipline already

noted amongst his troops, Heilmann's orders were practically ignored.

The 14 Fallschirm Regiment's initial advance was relatively uneventful. The men quickly overran the small American outposts on the west bank of the Our, but then encountered the stumbling block of Company I, III/110th, in Weiler, as well as artillery fire directed by an observer on the heights behind Wahlhausen. This was already a problem for Oberst Heinz Kokott's 26 Volksgrenadier Division, XLVII Panzer Korps, to their north, and the almost inevitable result was that Heilmann's paras became mixed up in Kokott's battle. Company I put up a game struggle against I/14 Bataillon, but was quickly surrounded and the survivors had to fight their way west through the woods to where fierce battles were soon raging at Holzthum and Consthum.

On 14 Fallschirm Regiment's left, II Bataillon now encountered a similar problem in Hoscheid, where Colonel Rudder had rushed what meagre reserves were left to him. The village's garrison nevertheless included six 105mm and three 75mm M4s from Company C, 707th Tank Battalion, and part of the 110th Regiment's anti-tank company. Lacking armoured support, because only a few of Hollunder's StuGs had so far managed to get across the Our over the top of a weir at Vianden, Heilmann's paras made an unsuccessful assault on the village during the night of the 16th/17th. They then encircled the village and tried again in the morning from the west while a

The advance of 5 Fallschirm Division's two leading regiments over December 17/19 with 352 Volksgrenadier Division to their south and 26 Volksgrenadier Division to the north. The 14 Regiment's assault on Wiltz itself was an unscheduled 'private venture'.

16/12/1944		17/12	18-19/12	20/12	21/12	22/12	23/12		24/12		25/12	26/12	27/12	28-29/12	30/12	31/12	1/1
pages 31-37,63-66,69-72		67-68		38-39		40-42	45-46,80-81		43-44,47-48		82-83		84-85		49-50		

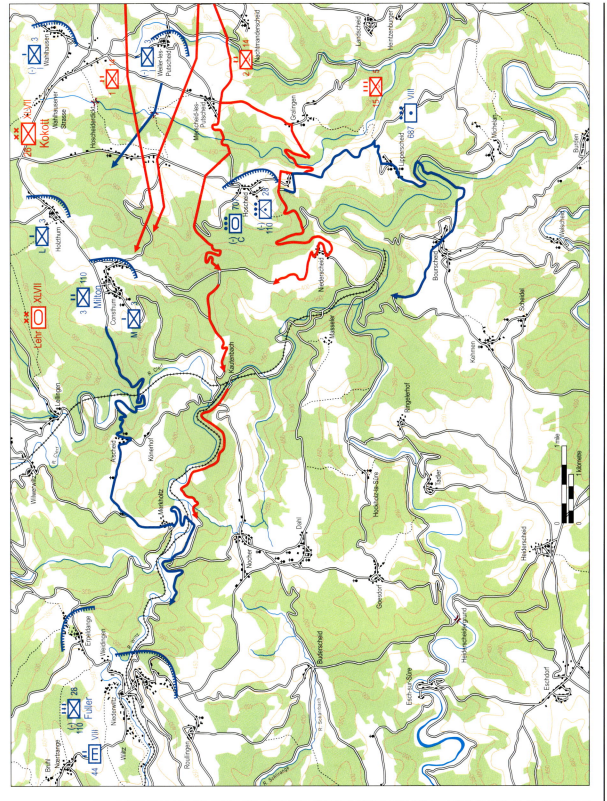

16/12/1944		17/12	18-19/12	20/12	21/12	22/12	23/12	24/12		25/12	26/12	27/12	28-29/12	30/12	31/12	1/1
pages 31-37,63-66,69-72		67-68		38-39		40-42	45-46,80-81	43-44,47-48	82-83		84-85		49-50			

A 7.5cm PaK 40 knocked out at some point during the advance. 5 Fallschirm Division's Panzerjäger Abteilung was still en route from Holland at the beginning of the battle but provided useful service during Patton's counter-attack. This crew knocked out two M4s before being silenced. (U.S. Signal Corps)

handful of StuGs gave covering fire from the north. It was an uneven battle and by late on the 17th the American tanks were running low on ammunition. As night fell the surviving infantry piled on to their deck plates and the tanks fought their way out south to Lipperscheid, where they found the 687th Field Artillery Battalion already pulling back west of the Clerf. The Hoscheid defenders followed suit, reinforcing the garrison in Wiltz. II/14 Fallschirm Regiment had lost over 100 men in the attack.

Meanwhile, the engineers had finally succeeded in completing a bridge over the Our at Roth. They had been delayed by bomb craters on the approach road, by harassing American artillery fire, and by their own inexperience, but at last it was done and Hollunder's StuGs, as well as the rest of 5 Fallschirm Division's vehicles and towed artillery, could join in the advance. On the right flank, 14 Fallschirm Regiment had become seriously disorganised during the mêlées at Weiler and Hoscheid, but Heilmann rallied the two leading battalions and pushed on to Kautenbach, where the pioniere who had fought alongside them quickly constructed a bridge over the Clerf.

Now, however, swept along in part by the momentum of XLVII Panzer Korps' advance on their right flank, 14 Fallschirm Regiment surged towards Wiltz. By this time, midday on December 18, Colonel Rudder's 109th Regiment had completely lost contact with the neighbouring 110th, and at his command post in Wiltz itself the American 28th Infantry Division's commander, Major-General Norman Cota, had already decided that any further defence east of the Clerf was impossible. Nor was any thought of a counter-attack feasible, given the meagre forces

available, unless Patton's Third Army to the south could come to VIII Corps' assistance. Cota therefore moved his command post back to Sibret, southwest of Bastogne, leaving command in Wiltz to his executive officer, Colonel Dan Strickler. The mainstay of the American defence was the 44th Engineer Combat Battalion, with stragglers coming in all the time from the 110th Regiment and a few from the 109th. It was actually survivors from Major Harold Milton's III/110th who provided the magnet for 14 Fallschirm Regiment, which followed in hot pursuit.

By this time, the tanks of Panzer 'Lehr' (XLVII Panzer Korps, Fifth Panzer Armee) had already bypassed Wiltz after a brief skirmish and the town was under attack from north and east by Kokott's 26 Volksgrenadier Division. 14 Fallschirm Regiment added its weight from the southeast and, assaulted from three directions, Colonel Strickler ordered the town evacuated, using the early nightfall as cover. It was no orderly retirement, because by this time the countryside between Wiltz and Bastogne was swarming with men from LXXXV and XLVII Korps, but about 200 GIs made it back to Sibret.

If they had hoped to find sanctuary they were disappointed because a company of 14 Fallschirm Regiment's men, hitching a ride with Major Rolf Kunkel's Aufklärungs Abteilung from 26 Volksgrenadier Division, overran the tiny garrison early on December 21, forcing General Cota to remove himself into Bastogne. By that night the paras had reached Senochamps, sealing the last road into or out of the town and opening the road west for Panzer 'Lehr'. The very next day, however, would see the beginning of Patton's counter-attack.

16/12/1944		17/12	18-19/12	20/12	21/12	22/12	23/12	24/12		25/12	26/12	27/12	28-29/12	30/12	31/12	1/1
pages 31-37,63-66,69-72		67-68		38-39		40-42	45-46,80-81	43-44,47-48		82-83		84-85		49-50		

LXXXV KORPS' BATTLES

15 Fallschirm Regiment

Vianden to Warnach – December 16–21

Oberstleutnant Kurt Gröschke's 15 Fallschirm Regiment's men moved without problem after their long journey from the division's assembly area at Bitburg into the foxholes vacated by 352 Volksgrenadier Division, and crossed the Our between Vianden and Roth without further difficulty in the pre-dawn darkness on December 16. There was little snow at present on this sector of the front because the last couple of days had seen mostly sleet and rain, and now river mist concealed the paras so they were able quickly to kill or capture all the men of Lieutenant Prazenka's Intelligence and Reconnaissance Platoon in the Hôtel Heintz in Vianden itself. Prazenka's tiny garrison, from Major William Maroney's 2nd Battalion of Colonel Rudder's 109th Infantry Regiment, was so taken by surprise that

he had no chance to radio a warning to Maroney, back in the battalion command post at Bastendorf. As a result, Gröschke's leading battalion reached the insignificant village of Walsdorf, some two miles west of the Our, without encountering any further opposition. This fortuitously put it smack in between Maroney's Company F on the Stolzembourg heights and Company E in Führen (Fouren). Company G and a battery of 105mm howitzers from the 107th Field Artillery Battalion lay behind them in Brandenburg.

Alerted by Seventh Armee's preliminary artillery barrage, Colonel Rudder moved Company G up on the right of Company F, replacing it in Brandenburg by Company C from the 109th's reserve 1st Battalion (Lieutenant-Colonel H. R. Williams), which was stationed in Diekirch. However, for some unexplained

Shortages of fuel and artillery ammunition were not the only problems encountered by the German armies involved in the Ardennes. Here, Fallschirmjäger strip the boots from dead U.S. soldiers. Pillaging was common on both sides throughout the war but all these paras were concerned about was keeping their feet dry since trench foot was another common problem in December 1944. Note the wartime censoring of the signpost.
(Author's collection)

16/12/1944		17/12	18-19/12	20/12	21/12	22/12	23/12	24/12	25/12	26/12	27/12	28-29/12	30/12	31/12	1/1
pages 28-30,34-37,63-66,69-72	67-68			38-39		40-42	45-46,80-81	43-44,47-48	82-83		84-85		49-50		

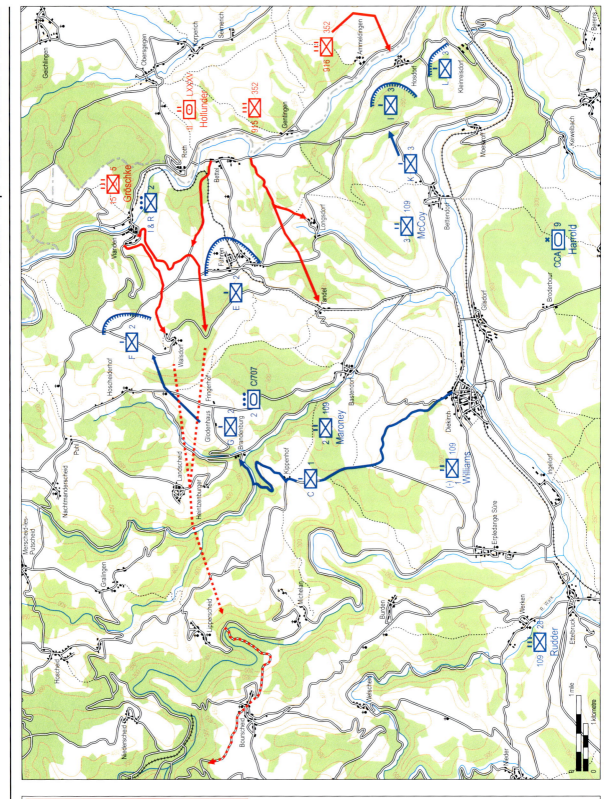

16/12/1944		17/12	18-19/12	20/12	21/12	22/12	23/12	24/12		25/12	26/12	27/12	28-29/12	30/12	31/12	1/1
pages 28-30,34-37,63-66,69-72	67-68		38-39			40-42	45-46,80-81	43-44,47-48	82-83		84-85			49-50		

Final resting place for one of 5 Fallschirm Division's men in a sun-dappled copse. Many veterans from earlier campaigns managed to retain their jump helmets while the replacements in their ranks had ordinary Stalhelme with Luftwaffe insignia, as seen in the previous photo. (U.S. Signal Corps)

reason Gröschke's leading battalion made no immediate attempt to exploit its advantage beyond firing ineffectually at the defenders in Führen, and merely waited in Walsdorf until the second battalion caught up with it later in the day. By this time, of course, the Americans knew they were facing a full-scale attack, but Colonel Rudder, back in the 109th's command post in Ettelbruck, had few reserves with which to meet it.

During the night, remembering his orders to avoid confrontation and leave American strongpoints to be mopped up by the reserve 13 Fallschirm Regiment, Gröschke took advantage of a wooded defile to continue advancing west in between the 109th's Companies F and G, but early on the 17th the 2nd Platoon from Company C, 707th Tank Battalion, moved into position to block the regiment. A couple of assault guns from 11 StuG Brigade which had joined up were knocked out by bazookas but the handful of M4s were no obstacle to the paras, who continued to infiltrate between and behind the two American companies. By daybreak on December 18 the GIs were completely cut off, even though they had not been attacked, and Colonel Rudder ordered them to fight their way out south to Diekirch, helped by the tank platoon. By this time LXXXV Korps' engineers had completed the bridge over the Our below Vianden at Roth, and the balance of the StuG Brigade had caught up with the Fallschirmjäger, along with their own trucks. The Panzerjäger Abteilung and mortar company, missing at the start of the offensive, also caught up and Gröschke's men now pressed on west to cross the

river Clerf below Lipperscheid. They had by this time driven a wedge completely in between the U.S. 109th and 110th Infantry Regiments, 28th Infantry Division, and were able to advance unopposed through Bourscheid and across the Sûre. Avoiding the temptation to get involved alongside 14 Fallschirm Regiment in the battle for Wiltz, Gröschke drove his men on along the north bank of the Sûre through Kaundorf, Boulaide and Tintange, and on December 21 reached the regiment's assigned destination at Martelange, on the main Arlon–Bastogne road. Here, engineers demolished a span of the bridge and Gröschke placed one of his companies in the terraced slopes overlooking the river, establishing his command post further back in the village of Warnach. 14 Fallschirm Regiment, meanwhile, having extricated itself from Wiltz, had moved in on his right between Sibret and Chaumont, with a forward outpost in Burnon; and now the divisional CO, Ludwig Heilmann, brought his reserve 13 Regiment up forward with one battalion in Boulaide and a second south of the Sûre at Bigonville. Next day, Patton's III Corps began its counter-attack, with CCA of 4th Armored Division attacking at Martelange, CCB through Burnon toward Chaumont and, later, CCR toward Bigonville. The scene was set for a classic encounter in which Heilmann's much-maligned paras were to acquit themselves well and deny Patton his wish to relieve the defenders in Bastogne by Christmas.

The first phase of 15 Fallschirm Regiment's advance separated Companies F and G of II/109th Infantry Battalion from the rest of the regiment, forcing them to fight their way out back to Diekirch, while on the paras' left flank 352 Volksgrenadier Division was involved in its own battles at Führen, Longsdorf and Tandel. After this, Gröschke's regiment, once its transport got across the Our at Roth, made almost record time reaching its objective at Martelange.

16/12/1944		17/12	18-19/12	20/12	21/12	22/12	23/12	24/12	25/12	26/12	27/12	28-29/12	30/12	31/12	1/1
pages 28-30,34-37,63-66,69-72		67-68		38-39		40-42	45-46,80-81	43-44,47-48	82-83		84-85		49-50		

LXXXV KORPS' BATTLES

915 Volksgrenadier Regiment

Führen – December 16–19

While 15 Fallschirm Regiment was able to bypass Führen, the village and its defenders lay on the immediate flank of 915 Volksgrenadier Regiment's planned route west toward Ettelbruck, and could not be ignored. The regiment, which had re-formed on the right flank of Generalmajor Erich Schmidt's 352 Volksgrenadier Division after surrendering its earlier foxholes to Heilmann's Fallschirmjäger, began to cross the Our around Bettel in the pre-dawn darkness on December 16.

Screened by the mist which aided all of Seventh Armee's assault companies, the leading two battalions fortuitously struck at the junction between the U.S. 109th Regiment's 2nd Battalion, whose Company E was in Führen, and the 3rd Battalion's Company I deployed in front of Bettendorf. There was a 2,000-yard (1,820m) gap in between the American positions which the Volksgrenadiers exploited, advancing unopposed through Longsdorf and Tandel. The first the American 3rd Battalion commander – Lieutenant-Colonel Jim McCoy – knew of the regiment's attack was when the Volksgrenadiers began firing into Battery A of the 108th Field Artillery Battalion to the east of Diekirch at around 1000 hrs.

Lieutenant-Colonel James Rudder, the 109th's CO, immediately drew on his meagre reserves and sent Companies A and B of Lieutenant-Colonel H. R. Williams' 1st Battalion (then in reserve in Diekirch) into a counter-attack. They were supported in this by the 1st Platoon, Company C, 707th Tank Battalion. Although progress was slow, by nightfall Company A was in sight of Longsdorf and Company B was overlooking Tandel. To their north, however, II/915 Volksgrenadier Bataillon had continued its advance and was by this time itself overlooking Bastendorf.

II/109th's Company E in Führen, commanded by Captain R.W. Cureton, was now completely cut off and

Colonel Rudder mustered what reserves he could to add their weight to the counter-attack, hoping to break through to the isolated company's relief. To this end he sent a platoon from Company A of the 103rd Engineer Combat Battalion and one from Company A of the 630th Tank Destroyer Battalion with 7.62mm guns to bolster Company A outside Longsdorf, and a second platoon of M4s towards Tandel.

During December 17, 915 Volksgrenadier Regiment's II Bataillon, aided by a battalion from 352 Division's reserve 914 Regiment, launched a series of attacks against Führen, but they were unco-ordinated, partly because the CO of 915 Regiment had been wounded and partly because the divisional commander, General Schmidt, had his hands full with the American counter-attacks at Longsdorf and Tandel. Company A was checked by mortar and machine-gun fire just short of the former village, but Company B recaptured Tandel. When it tried to advance further toward Führen, however, the company was caught by enfilading fire and forced to withdraw.

Now 915 Regiment's I Bataillon grenadiers, accompanied by two of the division's handful of Jagdpanzer 38(t)s, slipped through the gap between the two relief forces. They ambushed two of the 707th Tank Battalion's M4s and pushed on to the junction of the Tandel and Longsdorf roads. This, however, was defended by the 109th Anti-Tank Company and, although their little 57mm guns could make no impression on the Hetzers, the Americans also had a quick-firing 40mm Bofors, which caused heavy casualties amongst the grenadiers, forcing them to abandon the attack.

Elsewhere, however, 915 Regiment had itself been successful in stopping the American counter-attacks toward Führen. Company A was reduced to one officer and 25 men and Company B again could make

16/12/1944		17/12	18-19/12	20/12	21/12	22/12	23/12	24/12		25/12	26/12	27/12	28-29/12	30/12	31/12	1/1
pages 28-33,36-37,63-66,69-72	67-68			38-39		40-42	45-46,80-81	43-44,47-48		82-83		84-85		49-50		

no headway beyond Tandel. Although Captain Cureton's Company E was still holding on in Führen, greatly aided by artillery fire which repeatedly broke up the Volksgrenadiers' attacks, the men were running low on ammunition and food and a patrol sent from Tandel to resupply them failed to get through. On the American 3rd Battalion's north flank, meanwhile, II/915 had successfully bypassed Bastendorf and was assaulting the positions of both the 107th and 108th Field Artillery Battalions' Battery As. Rudder managed to assemble a scratch force of M4s to go to their aid, but the gun positions were no longer tenable and all the tanks could do was cover their withdrawal, which left Company E in Führen without support.

After an initially promising start which drove a wedge between the American II/ and III/109th Battalions, 915 Volksgrenadier Regiment's attack stalled at Longsdorf and Tandel in the face of counter-attacks, but once the defenders in Führen were subdued and 914 Regiment was able to add its weight to the centre of the division's attack, the Americans were forced back to Diekirch.

It was the end for Cureton's men. Their last radio message was timed at 2300 hrs. Then III/915 and I/914 Volksgrenadier Bataillonen launched a concerted attack on the village from two sides, better co-ordinated this time. On the morning of December 18 an M4 and a Jeep managed to creep unseen to the edge of Führen, but found Cureton's command post burned and no sign of any of his men.

The U.S. 109th Regiment's positions east of Diekirch could not be held any longer, and during the morning of December 18 what was left of Companies A and B, I/109th, withdrew from Tandel and Longsdorf to the road junction, which was defended by the anti-tank company. Here, the American official history states that they were attacked by two 'Mark VI tanks', an obvious impossibility since Seventh Armee had no tanks at all, let alone Tigers! Whatever these vehicles were, they were however successful in dislodging the roadblock, destroying all the anti-tank guns in the process and forcing the survivors back to Diekirch, where the remainder of II/ and III/109th were also re-assembling.

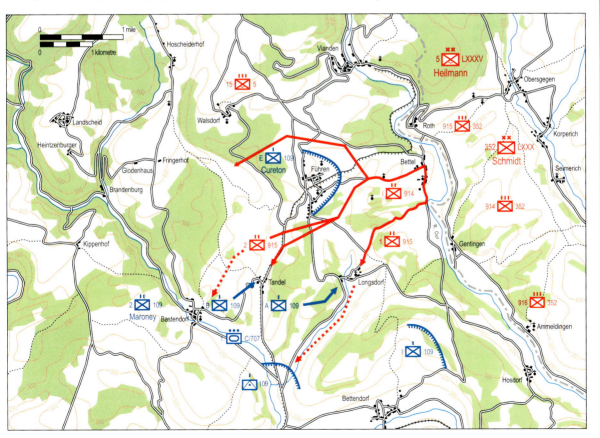

16/12/1944		17/12	18-19/12	20/12	21/12	22/12	23/12	24/12		25/12	26/12	27/12	28-29/12	30/12	31/12	1/1
pages 28-33,36-37,63-66,69-72	67-68			38-39		40-42	45-46,80-81	43-44,47-48		82-83		84-85		49-50		

35

LXXXV KORPS' BATTLES

916 Volksgrenadier Regiment

Hosdorf/Diekirch – December 16–20

Attacking on 915 Volksgrenadier Regiment's left flank south of Gentingen through Hosdorf, 916 Regiment of 352 Volksgrenadier Division was initially opposed by Companies I and L of Lieutenant-Colonel Jim McCoy's 3rd Battalion, 109th Infantry Regiment, deployed in front of Bettendorf between Longsdorf and Reisdorf.

The regiment's intended route was Bettendorf–Diekirch–Ettelbruck, with 276 Volksgrenadier Division, LXXX Korps, on its left flank. However, as it turned out, this was the most strongly defended position on the whole of LXXXV Korps' front since it dominated the heights overlooking the confluence of the rivers Our and Sûre/Sauer and had its right flank protected by the Sûre. The Volksgrenadiers could not, therefore, pass in between the American companies as their comrades to the north were able, but had to slog for a foothold over the Our at Hosdorf.

The 916 Regiment made no headway at all on December 16, being pinned to the steep river bank by American artillery fire. The Germans' own artillery barrage in this sector had been ineffectual; the defenders' positions and communications were still intact. On December 17, therefore, the divisional CO, General Schmidt, decided to try a different tactic and outflank Company L by moving 916 Volksgrenadier Regiment up the south bank of the Sûre through Reisdorf, encroaching on 276 Volksgrenadier Division's own battle against the U.S. 60th Armored Infantry Battalion. Again, however, the attempt was thwarted by the deadly fire of the American 107th and 108th Field Artillery Battalions and casualties amongst the grenadiers were very heavy. Help was at hand, though, for late in the day 915 Volksgrenadier Regiment's II Bataillon forced the American artillery batteries to withdraw.

Daybreak on December 18 brought hope to 916 Regiment, for not only had Führen finally been captured but the Americans were also pulling back from Longsdorf. A determined assault on the American 3rd Battalion's left flank northwest of Hosdorf overran a platoon of Company K, which had been sent to reinforce the initial two companies. With his 2nd Battalion now in full – albeit disciplined – retreat, the situation of the 3rd Battalion had become precarious, and all three companies were in danger of being encircled. Colonel Rudder was therefore forced to order their own withdrawal through Bettendorf to Diekirch after blowing the bridge over the Sûre at Bettendorf to delay any possible outflanking attack on

The expressions on the faces of these two tankers from the U.S. 109th Infantry Regiment's attached 707th Tank Battalion show the weariness of their struggle against 352 Volksgrenadier Division. (U.S. Army)

16/12/1944	17/12	18-19/12	20/12	21/12	22/12	23/12	24/12	25/12	26/12	27/12	28-29/12	30/12	31/12	1/1
pages 28-35,63-66,69-72	67-68		38-39		40-42	45-46,80-81	43-44,47-48	82-83		84-85		49-50		

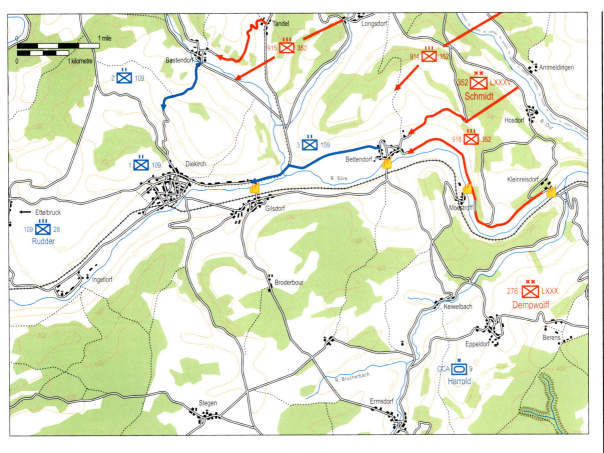

After finally achieving a breakthrough on the northern flank of the U.S. III/109th on the heights west of Hosdorf, 916 Volksgrenadier Regiment pursued them back to Diekirch and ultimately to Ettelbruck.

Diekirch from the south bank of the river. By early evening, therefore, 916 Volksgrenadier Regiment had command of the heights in the Our/Sûre triangle and, with 914 Regiment taking up its place in the centre of the division's line, could begin to make more headway.

The American 109th Regiment, with Colonel Rudder's command post back in Ettelbruck, was now formed in an arc in front of Diekirch. However, it was a sadly depleted regiment. Over 500 officers and men had been killed or captured, the anti-tank company had been wiped out and the few surviving M4s of the 707th Tank Battalion had precious little ammunition or fuel left. So far, 352 Volksgrenadier Division was handsomely repaying Colonel Rudder for his audacity on 'Omaha' beach.

However, his men had a respite for most of

December 19 while General Schmidt reorganised his regiments for the assault on Diekirch. He was also at last able to bring his artillery across the Our and as the afternoon wore on pounded the 109th's positions while 916 Regiment launched a series of assaults from the east and elements of 915 Regiment from the north. These failed to break through the American perimeter, but Rudder informed his divisional commander, General Cota, that Diekirch was essentially indefensible and that the whole regiment could be lost unless it was allowed to retire behind the river Alzette, anchoring its flank on Ettelbruck.

Even before he received permission to withdraw, Rudder had already begun the process. Parties of engineers sowed mines behind the long column of infantry while German artillery shells continued to burst amongst them. Other engineers, protected by a rearguard from Company C of the 707th Tank Battalion, blew the bridges in Diekirch and the American regiment re-assembled south of Ettelbruck to await 352 Volksgrenadier Division's next assault.

16/12/1944		17/12	18-19/12	20/12	21/12	22/12	23/12	24/12		25/12	26/12	27/12	28-29/12	30/12	31/12	1/1
pages 28-35,63-66,69-72		67-68		38-39		40-42	45-46,80-81	43-44,47-48		82-83		84-85		49-50		

LXXXV KORPS' BATTLES

915 Volksgrenadier Regiment

Ettelbruck/Grosbous – December 20–25

After the U.S. 109th Infantry Regiment evacuated Diekirch, 916 Volksgrenadier Regiment moved in to occupy the town. Finding one bridge still sufficiently intact to carry infantry and one field gun at a time, the regiment then crossed to the south bank of the Sûre with the intention of attacking Ettelbruck from the left flank. Similarly, 915 Volksgrenadier Regiment, which had re-assembled west of Bastendorf, crossed the river north of the town and marched to the river Wark, intending to envelop the defenders from the northwest. 914 Regiment, in the centre, formed the divisional reserve. Meanwhile, in order to give General Schmidt's 352 Volksgrenadier Division a bit more muscle, Erich Brandenberger sent a column of heavier artillery and Nebelwerfers from Armee reserve to Bastendorf.

At his command post in Ettelbruck itself, Colonel Rudder had also been busy. He placed his 1st Battalion in and either side of the town itself, with the 2nd Battalion on its left covering the south bank of the Wark, and the 3rd to the south, similarly covering the stretch of the river Alzette in front of Bissen. At the same time, engineers demolished all the bridges in Ettelbruck. General Schmidt also drove his men hard and, during the 21st, 915 and 916 Regiments converged on Ettelbruck from north and south. Against such superior odds, under heavy artillery fire and in danger of being encircled, during the night Rudder withdrew his three battalions southwest and established a new, shorter, defensive perimeter in front of Vichten.

December 22 began well for 352 Volksgrenadier Division but then the situation rapidly disintegrated as Patton's Third Army began its counter-attack. Advancing on the right of the U.S. III Corps with the river Alzette offering some protection to its right flank, Major-General Horace McBride's 80th Infantry

Division marched rapidly north either side of Bissen and relieved Colonel Rudder's 109th at Vichten. On the 80th's left, Major-General Willard Paul's 26th Infantry Division was advancing on a broader front, but 352 Volksgrenadier Division very quickly encountered both.

Early on the morning of the 22nd, 915 Volksgrenadier Regiment began moving west along the Merzig road and I Bataillon in the van soon reached Grosbous, while a reconnaissance party got as far west as Pratz. Following more slowly behind, II Bataillon and the accompanying artillery were marching in an almost parade ground column, confident that there was no enemy in front of them. Nor was there, but Colonel William Taylor's 319th Infantry Regiment, 80th Infantry Division, was approaching unobserved from the southwest. II/915 was caught napping and the American regiment sliced through the tail of the column before the grenadiers could re-form in a battle line. In a state of understandable confusion, the remainder of the battalion nevertheless quickly formed a defensive perimeter in Merzig, but the GIs did not pursue their advantage and continued heading north towards the river Sûre.

Meanwhile, further east, 914 Volksgrenadier Regiment was approaching Ettelbruck when artillery observers spotted a long column of men advancing up the Alzette valley from the south. This was actually Colonel Lansing McVickar's 318th Infantry Regiment, which quickly went to ground when the artillery massed at Bastendorf opened fire. 914 Volksgrenadier Regiment hastily moved in to occupy Ettelbruck itself and the high ground just to the west. During that night and the following day the Americans launched several assaults which failed to dislodge the defenders, and the grenadiers inflicted such heavy casualties that the American divisional commander

16/12/1944		17/12	18-19/12	20/12	21/12	22/12	23/12	24/12	25/12	26/12	27/12	28-29/12	30/12	31/12	1/1
pages 28-37,63-66,69-72		67-68				40-42	45-46,80-81	43-44,47-48	82-83		84-85		49-50		

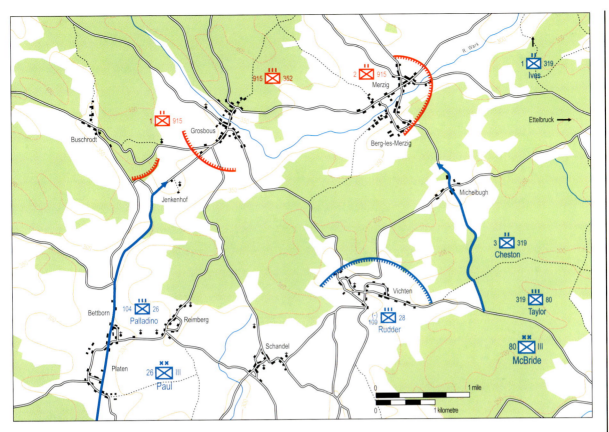

915 Volksgrenadier Regiment's leading two battalions were isolated by the U.S. III Corps' rapid advance on December 22 and although the men put up a determined resistance, their plight was hopeless.

called the assault off. For the next 24 hours he simply plastered the town with 105 and 155mm shells. This barrage was so sustained that Schmidt pulled the survivors out during the night of the 24th/25th, and an American battalion promptly moved into the ruins of the town.

Returning to 915 Volksgrenadier Regiment, now cut off from friendly lines in two enclaves at Grosbous and Merzig, it was I Bataillon in the former village which faced the American 26th Infantry Division whose 104th Regiment commanded by Lieutenant-Colonel Jack Palladino neared the grenadiers' positions during the morning of December 22. The German battalion charged from the woods south of Grosbous to hit the leading American companies with such force that they reeled back in disorder. However, once again American artillery was quickly in action,

forcing the grenadiers to retire in haste. The bulk of the American regiment pushed on north through Grosbous itself, leaving just an infantry company to keep an eye on the woods. I/915 Volksgrenadier Bataillon was not finished yet, though, and launched a series of attacks during December 23 which forced Palladino to send a second company of infantry supported by tank destroyers to their aid.

During the same morning, unluckily, the CO of the U.S. 319th Infantry Regiment, 80th Infantry Division, had ordered his reserve 3rd Battalion to attack II/915 Bataillon in Merzig. Here the depleted battalion was only able to put up a token resistance and although a few escaped, the majority surrendered. It was a similar story with I/915 Bataillon in the woods around Grosbous.

The American reinforcements proved decisive and although the grenadiers held out during Christmas Eve, once they were out of ammunition the survivors gave up the struggle and headed back east during the night. About 200 men finally managed to rejoin the division over the next couple of days.

16/12/1944		17/12	18-19/12	20/12	21/12	22/12	23/12	24/12	25/12	26/12	27/12	28-29/12	30/12	31/12	1/1
pages 28-37,63-66,69-72		67-68				40-42	45-46,80-81	43-44,47-48	82-83		84-85		49-50		

LXXXV KORPS' BATTLES
13 and 15 Fallschirm Regiments

Warnach/Bigonville – December 22–24

Visiting Oberstleutnant Kurt Gröschke's new command post in Warnach on the evening of December 21, Ludwig Heilmann could be quietly proud of 5 Fallschirm Division's achievements over the past five days. His men had kept pace with those of XLVII Panzer Korps on his right flank, reached their assigned blocking positions south of Bastogne, and far outstripped the other three divisions in Seventh Armee. Gröschke's 15 Regiment was digging in to present a defence in depth along the main road from Arlon up which Patton was expected to launch his main counter-attack, and the paras had the support of Oberst Hollunder's attached 11 Sturmgeschutz Brigade. To their west, 14 Fallschirm Regiment was similarly digging in between Remonville, on the Neufchâteau–Bastogne road, and Hollange, with its command post further back in Chaumont; and 13 Fallschirm Regiment, the divisional reserve, was moving up to take up station on the left with its forward battalion in Bigonville. This lay on the south bank of the Sûre but conveniently blocked the minor road leading from Martelange towards Harlange. If the Allies broke through here, they would have access to the spider's web of roads southeast of Bastogne which would double the difficulties of further defence.

Heilmann's principal worry, this evening of December 21, was the wide gap which had developed between his own men and those of 352 Volksgrenadier Division, still battling miles to the east in the Ettelbruck sector. Fortunately, although he did not know it until the next day, help was on its way. The Heeresgruppe B commander, Walter Model, had already seen the danger of 5 Fallschirm Division's exposed position and was preparing orders to release the powerful Führer Grenadier Brigade from reserve, plus 79 Volksgrenadier Division. At this point Heilmann's division would be transferred from LXXXV to LIII Korps whose commander, General Friedrich-Wilhelm von Rothkirch, by establishing his command post in Wiltz would be able to exercise much closer control over the next phase of the battle than could Baptist Kniess back in Diekirch.

The first sight Gröschke's forward company in the riverside village of Martelange had of the enemy was a troop of light tanks accompanied by a skirmish line of infantry approaching from the south. These were actually M5s and combat engineers from Brigadier-General Herbert Earnest's Combat Command A of 4th Armored Division. Gröschke's men had no orders to try to stop the Americans in Martelange, and contented themselves with pouring harassing fire into the engineers surveying the damage to the bridge; then, as darkness fell, they pulled back to a better defensive line on a ridge just south of Warnach, leaving a squad of men with a radio operator to keep an eye on events.

As it happened, it was not until late the following afternoon, December 23, that the American engineers completed assembly of a Bailey bridge but then, led by M4s of the 35th Tank Battalion, General Earnest's men began crossing in strength. Gröschke's forward company opened fire as the tanks – their decks packed with infantry – approached the ridge. Much to the paras' surprise, the column stopped, but the reason soon became obvious as 105mm shells began crashing down amongst the trees, and Gröschke

The twin battles for Warnach and Bigonville over December 23-24 were almost copybook exercises, each following a very similar pattern. In both cases the Fallschirmjäger proved far more stubborn than their training and experience would have indicated but, without any tanks of their own, at the end of the day they were overwhelmed.

16/12/1944		17/12	18-19/12	20/12	21/12	22/12	23/12	24/12		25/12	26/12	27/12	28-29/12	30/12	31/12	1/1
pages 28-37,63-66,69-72		67-68		38-39			45-46,80-81	43-44,47-48		82-83		84-85		49-50		

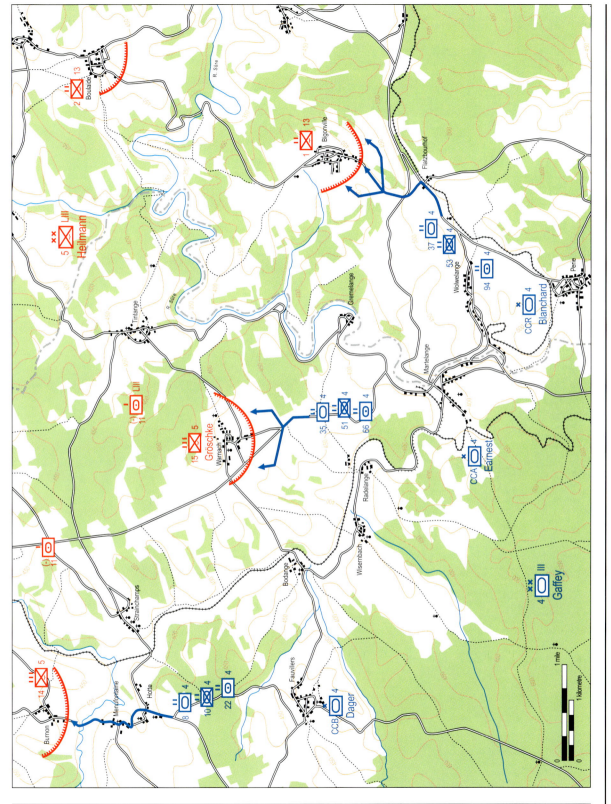

16/12/1944		17/12	18-19/12	20/12	21/12	22/12	23/12	24/12		25/12	26/12	27/12	28-29/12	30/12	31/12	1/1
pages 28-37,63-66,69-72		67-68		38-39				45-46, 80-81	43-44,47-48	82-83		84-85		49-50		

ordered his men to pull back into Warnach itself.

Meanwhile, that same afternoon a second column of American tanks was approaching Bigonville, where I/13 Fallschirm Regiment was deployed with its forward company lining the edge of a wood covering the road junction a mile south of the village. Pioniere had also sown a minefield in front of them. As the column – Colonel Wendell Blanchard's Combat Command R from 4th Armored Division – came into range, the paras opened a fusilade of fire which sent the GIs diving for cover. This time, the wily German commander knew what was coming next, and even before the artillery shells began descending he had begun pulling his men back. The hour-long barrage demolished a lot of trees but did little other damage, although a few men were not quick enough in retreating and got caught. As soon as the artillery fire stopped, the paras rapidly re-occupied their former positions and opened fire on the Americans as they climbed back into their half-tracks. Blanchard now decided to use his M4s (from the 37th Tank Battalion) to clear the wood, but they ran straight into the minefield and, as it was getting dark, Blanchard called off the attack until daylight.

Back in the 15 Fallschirm Regiment sector, however, Earnest tried to take Warnach by a surprise night attack. Gröschke's paras, supported by a company of StuGs (the other had gone to help 14 Fallschirm Regiment in Chaumont), easily repelled the first assault by M5s of A Troop, 25th Cavalry Reconnaissance Squadron. Earnest tried again, this time using a company of M4s, but most of the tanks got bogged down in a marsh and provided good targets for Hollunder's StuGs as day broke. Now, however, the American attack began in earnest. Two companies of M4s and one of M18s, each closely followed by a dismounted company of infantry, closed in on the village from east, west and south. Hollunder's StuGs put paid to four tanks and a Panzerfaust accounted for a fifth, but the American infantry were soon in the village itself, where a ferocious house-to-house battle lasted all morning. Gröschke's paras were not prepared to give up easily and every time the GIs captured a house, they counter-attacked. In the end, the Americans had to use the M4s to pour high explosive rounds into each house before they could make any headway. However, it was an uneven battle and at about midday Gröschke ordered a retreat, the men giving disciplined covering fire as they leapfrogged back into the shelter of the woods in the direction of Tintange. By this time the battalion was barely at company strength, having lost over 100 men killed or wounded and a similar number captured.

It was much the same story with I/13 Fallschirm Regiment in Bigonville on Christmas Eve. American engineers had cleared the minefield during the night, and at daybreak Colonel Blanchard organised two assault teams, each comprising a company of M4s and a company of armoured infantry, which attacked the village from east and west after a short artillery barrage. Here, lacking any StuGs to tackle the tanks, the paras waited until the Americans were actually in the village before opening up at point-blank range. Once again the battle disintegrated into a one-on-one mêlée with bayonets and grenades while the M4s poured fire into each house, setting many wooden-framed structures ablaze. However, the end came suddenly after one of the American teams broke right through to the northern edge of the village, blocking the para battalion's line of retreat to the river Sûre. Although a few men escaped through the woods, the majority of the survivors were forced to surrender. However, the Americans did not pursue their advantage. Patton had decided that battling through 5 Fallschirm Division was too costly and time-consuming, so Blanchard was ordered to vacate the hard-won village and move west to Neufchâteau to attempt another attack on 4th Armored Division's other flank. For the remainder of 13 Fallschirm Regiment, this provided a badly needed respite.

Until the arrival of the Führer Grenadier Brigade with 5 Fallschirm Division's transfer from LXXXV to LIII Korps, the paras had no armoured support apart from the 20 StuG IIIs of Oberst Hollunder's so-called 11 Sturmgeschutz 'Brigade'. (Imperial War Museum)

16/12/1944		17/12	18-19/12	20/12	21/12	22/12	23/12	24/12		25/12	26/12	27/12	28-29/12	30/12	31/12	1/1
pages 28-37,63-66,69-72		67-68		38-39			45-46, 80-81	43-44,47-48		82-83		84-85		49-50		

LXXXV KORPS' BATTLES
I/208 and I/212 Volksgrenadier Regiments

Eschdorf/Heiderscheid – December 24

Recognising that 5 Fallschirm Division was out on a limb and, although 352 Volksgrenadier Division had finally captured Diekirch, that a wide and dangerous gap had opened between the two divisions, Heeresgruppe B commander Walter Model re-assigned the former to LIII Korps on December 22 and reinforced it with the Führer Grenadier Brigade. At the same time he also released Oberst Alois Weber's understrength and poorly equipped 79 Volksgrenadier Division from reserve and assigned it to Kniess' LXXXV Korps. It duly began moving into place on the north flank of 352 Volksgrenadier Division during December 23 and was almost immediately thrown into action against the 80th Infantry Division from Patton's III Corps.

Like all the reinforcements sent to the front, Weber encountered the usual problems of traffic jams in the rear areas but, following on the heels of the Führer Grenadier Brigade (which crossed the Our at Roth) he took his leading battalions across the bridge further south at Gentingen. By nightfall on December 23, however, during a day which had seen FGB furiously engaged at Eschdorf and Heiderscheid, all that had arrived for the planned counter-attack on Christmas Eve were his 208 Regiment and I Bataillon of the 212th. The rest of the 212th, and 266 Regiment, were assembling further east around Bourscheid, which had been designated the divisional command post. Weber's artillery was miles behind and, although he had the support of the FGB's StuG Kompanie since his own division lacked any, it was a weak force with which to engage an enemy vastly stronger in matériel and manpower. But two companies from the Führer Grenadier Brigade had been cut off at Grevils-Brésil and were believed to be fighting their way back to the east, and it was hoped to rescue them as well as drive the enemy from Heiderscheid.

What was immediately obvious was that, in addition to trying to force armoured columns through to the relief of Bastogne, Patton was attempting to exploit the gap between 352 Volksgrenadier and 5 Fallschirm Divisions, driving a wedge of infantry from the 26th and 80th Infantry Divisions between them up to the Sûre and beyond. If Weber could not stop them, it was his duty to at least delay them as long as possible – a task he cannot have faced with equanimity given the lack of training or experience amongst his men. The first job was to evict the enemy from Heiderscheid, which they had captured the day before.

Weber assembled his two I Bataillonen behind the Führer Grenadier Brigade near Eschdorf, together with their Sturmgeschütze and some of FGB's SdKfz 251/17s with 20mm Flak guns, and launched his attack on Heiderscheid an hour before dawn after a ten-minute artillery barrage. The village was only weakly defended by Colonel Bandy's 2nd Battalion, 319th Infantry Regiment. This had reached Heiderscheid in the early hours of December 23, captured it after a fierce fight with elements of the Führer Grenadier Brigade during which the brigade commander, Hans-Joachim Kahler, had been wounded, and repulsed two counter-attacks later in the day. III/319th, which hurried to Bandy's assistance after recapturing Merzig from II/915 Volksgrenadier Regiment, found it was not needed and continued northeast towards Tadler, while I/319th headed for Kehmen on the road to Bourscheid.

The American battalion had been badly dented during the fighting on the 23rd and on the morning of Christmas Eve only had one rifle company in Heiderscheid itself, the other two having been sent to keep the bridge over the Sûre at Heiderscheidergrund under observation. But, as on so many other occasions during Seventh Armee's operations, this

16/12/1944		17/12	18-19/12	20/12	21/12	22/12	23/12	24/12		25/12	26/12	27/12	28-29/12	30/12	31/12	1/1
pages 28-37,63-66,69-72		67-68		38-39			40-42	45-46, 80-81	47-48	82-83		84-85		49-50		

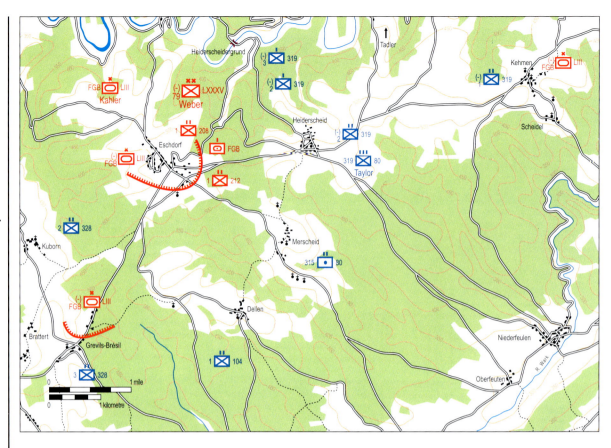

Assembling his leading two battalions just to the north of Eschdorf late on December 23 while the remainder of 79 Volksgrenadier Division was concentrated around Bourscheid to the east, Alois Weber launched his attack on Heiderscheid before dawn on Christmas Eve but had his men blown away by American artillery fire.

turned out to be enough because artillery was available to give support to Bandy's men.

As stated, Weber launched his assault an hour before dawn after a ten-minute bombardment, having rounded up a stray battery from 5 Fallschirm Division. The Führer Grenadier Brigade's StuGs and SdKfz 251s spearheaded the attack and quickly knocked out the sole Sherman guarding the western approach to the village.

The only other support Bandy's battalion might have had was a single tank destroyer, but its firing mechanism had been damaged by a stray bomb dropped during the night. Fortunately for the Americans, the FGB armour, lacking proper direction because of Kahler's injury, did not assault Heiderscheid itself. Instead, the vehicles raced up and down the south side of the village, pouring fire into the houses while remaining safely outside bazooka range. Then a second American tank appeared, shot up four of the Brigade's vehicles and caused the rest to fall back to Eschdorf. This left the main attack down to Weber's two grenadier battalions.

Twice during the morning his men managed to get close enough to hurl grenades through house windows but the return fire was devastating and, once the bulk of Weber's two battalions got into the village, the artillery observer from the American 315th Field Artillery Battalion called for supporting fire. It was a risky call, but Bandy's GIs did have some protection from the thick stone walls of the houses, whereas Weber's grenadiers were out in the open. For half an hour 155mm shells rained down in and around Heiderscheid, miraculously leaving the spire of the church intact but taking a heavy toll of Weber's men. He had no option but to recall them, but they left behind 76 dead and 26 too badly wounded to be moved.

16/12/1944	17/12	18-19/12	20/12	21/12	22/12	23/12	24/12	25/12	26/12	27/12	28-29/12	30/12	31/12	1/1
pages 28-37,63-66,69-72	67-68		38-39		40-42	45-46, 80-81	47-48	82-83	84-85		49-50			

LXXXV KORPS' BATTLES
266 and II/212 Volksgrenadier Regiments

Welscheid/Kehmen – December 23–January 1

Even before 79 Volksgrenadier Division was released from reserve on December 22, Patton's III Corps had made deep inroads into the partial vacuum in Seventh Armee's lines caused by the fact that the bulk of 352 Volksgrenadier Division was stalled at Ettelbruck with one of its regiments isolated around Grosbous and Merzig to the west. Ludwig Heilmann's 5 Fallschirm Division could not help because it had its own hands full with 4th Armored Division, so, while the Führer Grenadier Brigade began straggling piecemeal into the Arsdorf–Heiderscheid sector, Model wanted to create a 'backstop' in the densely wooded triangle formed by the long loop in the river Sûre at its confluence with the river Wiltz north of Bourscheid. The rugged terrain in this sector clearly favoured the defender, since it was virtually impassable to tanks except along the narrow roads, while digging in on reverse slopes would give a good measure of protection against artillery fire. Apart from his attempted rescue mission at Heiderscheid, therefore, the Bourscheid front was entrusted to Alois Weber's men, even though they had precious little artillery yet with which to help break up American infantry attacks.

Patton, of course, could see the same situation, so, while the 319th Regiment of 80th Infantry Division was battling towards the Sûre around Heiderscheid, and the 318th was keeping 352 Volksgrenadier Division pinned east of Ettelbruck, he ordered Major-General Horace McBride to release his reserve 317th Regiment to move in and take the ground before Seventh Armee got its own men there. Model, however, had moved more quickly than Patton, and even while Lieutenant-Colonel Henry Fisher's 317th was moving up the Alzette–Sûre river valley past Ettelbruck toward Welscheid, Weber had got a battalion of 266 Volksgrenadier Regiment covering the direct approach

at the loop in the river Wark which parallels that in the Sûre, with the second battalion poised to move into Kehmen the moment the American 1st Battalion there vacated it; and II/212 digging in on the heights overlooking the same loop west of Burden. Amongst other things, Weber calculated that his attack from Eschdorf towards Heiderscheid on Christmas Eve would force the Americans to pull back from both Kehmen and Tadler (III/319th) to help Bandy's 2nd Battalion. In fact, I/319th vacated Kehmen even earlier and even though III/319th pulled out of Tadler in response to the 2nd Battalion's plight, they reoccupied the village once II/319th appeared out of danger.

The men of 266 Volksgrenadier Regiment at Welscheid spotted the leading companies of Fisher's II/317th silhouetted against the snow by the bright moonlight as they cautiously approached the river Wark during the night of December 23. Mortars and sustained-fire MG42s were well emplaced to cover all the approaches to Welscheid, and now they opened up, forcing the Americans to dive for cover. The GIs remained pinned there throughout Christmas Eve, but eventually managed to retire when clouds obscured the moon during the night.

Meanwhile, Weber moved II/266 Volksgrenadier Bataillon into Kehmen the moment the American I/319th vacated it as he had planned, and took advantage of the high ground to emplace his few artillery pieces with a commanding field of fire over the whole valley of the Wark. This paid dividends because Colonel Fisher next tried to outflank Welscheid from the east by sending his 1st Battalion, 317th, towards Burden. Again, Weber's machine-gunners dug in behind the ridge had a field day as the American infantry came out of the woods, while the artillery and a handful of FGB StuGs at Kehmen poured high explosive into their ranks. The GIs fell back in total

16/12/1944		17/12	18-19/12	20/12	21/12	22/12	23/12	24/12	25/12	26/12	27/12	28-29/12	30/12	31/12	1/1
pages 28-37,63-66,69-72		67-68		38-39			40-42	80-81	43-44,47-48	82-83		84-85		49-50	

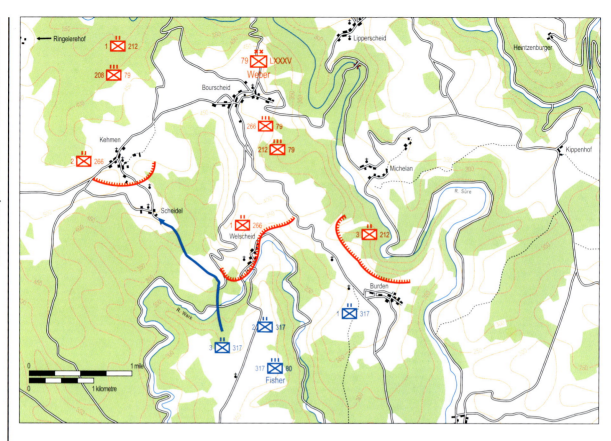

The excellent defensive nature of the landscape in what the Americans called the 'Bourscheid Triangle' can clearly be seen, but Weber's battle here still denied Patton the swift victory he had hoped for.

disorder leaving many dead behind and carrying 197 wounded.

On Christmas Day Colonel Fisher decided to try to get round Welscheid from the west, aiming to take out Weber's artillery at Kehmen. This time he used both his 3rd Battalion and the survivors from the 1st. Crossing the Wark well out of sight of the defenders in Welscheid, they hit the Kehmen-Welscheid road and very quickly overran the company of 266 Volksgrenadier Regiment in the tiny hamlet of Scheidel, but encountered exactly the same problem as in the preceding two attacks as they neared Kehmen. II/266 was well dug in with marksmen as well as machine-guns and the artillery on the high ground behind the village and the American assault faltered to a standstill. Fisher recalled his men, but again they carried 200 wounded with them. Weber's counter-attack at Heiderscheid may have failed, but he

had amply repaid the 80th Division.

On both sides, Christmas Day was one for reflection. Senior officers all recognised that the battle had changed shape and was about to enter a new phase. Model, while planning further attacks towards Bastogne, was also pulling his Panzer spearheads back and reassigning new tasks. He was also, although without letting the Führer know, planning a fall-back line, in which Weber's 79 Volksgrenadier Division would play a not insignificant part.

This sector of the front remained relatively quiet until the middle of January. The 80th Infantry Division was unable to make headway even while elsewhere the Americans were making rapid progress. The 'crunch' did not come until January 19 when the 5th Infantry Division recaptured Diekirch, putting itself between the Sûre and the Our. The Americans were also pressing in on Wiltz, and both moves threatened to encircle 79 Volksgrenadier Division. On the 21st Weber began withdrawing his men east toward the Our, but they could be proud of having held their sector for almost a full month.

16/12/1944	17/12	18-19/12	20/12	21/12	22/12	23/12	24/12	25/12	26/12	27/12	28-29/12	30/12	31/12	1/1
pages 28-37,63-66,69-72	67-68	38-39	40-42		80-81		43-44,47-48	82-83		84-85		49-50		

LXXXV KORPS' BATTLES

208 and I/212 Volksgrenadier Regiments

Ringelerhof – December 24–30

In the early hours of the morning of December 24, the American 1st Battalion, 319th Infantry Regiment, which had occupied Kehmen after a short battle with the Führer Grenadier Brigade, began marching west. Alois Weber had not lured them away as planned by his counter-attack at Heiderscheid; instead, the battalion was under fresh orders to occupy Ringelerhof, to the east of Tadler, as the CO of the 319th, Colonel William Taylor, wanted to bring his whole regiment up to the river Sûre. Regardless of the reason, it was just what Weber wanted, and II/266 Volksgrenadier Regiment promptly occupied the village as we have already seen. Nor, as it happened, did I/319th ever reach Ringelerhof. A couple of miles west of Kehmen the battalion was stalled by a single tank from the Führer Grenadier Brigade sitting at a road junction and even when this was eventually knocked out by a tank destroyer, the battalion was ordered to remain where it was to prevent the 2nd Battalion in Heiderscheid being surrounded during 79 Volksgrenadier Division's attack from Eschdorf.

The importance of Ringelerhof, or 'Ringel Hill' as the Americans called it, lay in its dominating position overlooking a wide bend in the Sûre. This was why Colonel Taylor wanted to seize it. Weber also wanted to hold it to secure his right flank but, with three battalions missing at Eschdorf, could only put a token force on to the hill. On Christmas morning, III/319th, which had been pulled back from Tadler to help II/319th if needed at Heiderscheid, returned to the village. Then the 90th Field Artillery Battalion fired a few rounds into the grenadiers who could be seen moving about on top of the hill, and the two companies of II/319th which had not been engaged at Heiderscheid moved through Tadler and chased Weber's small outpost off the heights.

The Seventh Armee commander, General Brandenberger, particularly wanted control of Ringelerhof as a prelude potentially for using the 'Bourscheid Triangle' as the launch pad for an attack northwest towards Bastogne in support of the main attack to be made by XXXIX Korps of Fifth Panzer Armee at the end of the month. To this end he loaned Weber a battalion of pioniere from Armee reserve. Unfortunately, there had been a complete breakdown in communications, or perhaps Weber was not yet aware that the Americans had captured the hill, because on Christmas morning the commander of the engineer battalion marched his men in column of twos confidently up the hill as though they were on a route march. They were rapidly disillusioned when machine-guns opened up on them, and fell back with heavy casualties.

Weber now badly needed to recapture Ringelerhof to safeguard his right flank and, with 208 and I/212 Regiments reunited with the rest of the division after their foray at Heiderscheid, he sent a battalion – which one is unclear – in to retake the hill shortly before midnight. Unfortunately, they were spotted, and the combined fire of four American artillery battalions broke the attack up before it had really started. With unusual humour, the U.S. official history states that the few grenadiers who got close to the village were met by 'the whistling ricochet of armour-piercing shells fired by a single tank destroyer that rushed around the village like a man stamping out a lawn fire'!

For the next four days the Bourscheid sector remained static, with the three regiments of the American 80th Infantry Division (minus two battalions which had gone to assist 4th Armored Division at Bastogne) contenting themselves with digging in. By this time, too, Weber's men were also well entrenched and, although the American artillery continued to pound their positions day and night, they suffered few

16/12/1944		17/12	18-19/12	20/12	21/12	22/12	23/12	24/12	25/12	26/12	27/12	28-29/12	30/12	31/12	1/1
pages 28-37,63-66,69-72		67-68		38-39		40-42	45-46,80-81	43-44	82-83		84-85		49-50		

casualties. Weber's main problem was his own lack of artillery, for the bulk of the weapons in Seventh Armee's Volks-Artillerie and Volks-Werfer batteries had either gone to LIII or LXXX Korps. Nevertheless, Brandenberger continued to pressure him into retaking Ringelerhof and to this end he assembled both battalions of 208 Regiment and I/212 Regiment for a full-blown assault on December 30.

Under normal circumstances, the attack should have succeeded because by this time Ringelerhof was merely defended by a single company, E Company of II/319th. Unfortunately, the Americans were

The map shows the overall situation between December 25 and 30 with Weber's final attack against Ringelerhof arrowed. What is surprising seen at this scale is that McBride made no attempt to exploit the central Kehmen route from the west. The explanation is that he had lost two battalions of his 318th Regiment to reinforce 4th Armored Division, and the third was tied down at Ettelbruck to the southeast.

forewarned by a prisoner captured by a patrol the previous evening, and were ready and waiting with no fewer than nine field artillery battalions poised to give support. Even so, Weber's assault almost worked. His men assembled out of sight at the edge of the woods below the crest of the hill and charged forward in the pre-dawn darkness so quickly that they were into the village before the Americans could sound the alarm. A number of grenadiers actually got to Lieutenant-Colonel Paul Bandy's 2nd Battalion command post before they were driven back almost single-handed by Pfc W.J. McKenzie. (McKenzie also took 16 prisoners and was later awarded the DSC for his part in this action.) At the end of the day, however, it was the American artillery which as usual proved decisive. As at Heiderscheid, Weber's grenadiers were out in the open when the 105 and 155mm shells began raining down. Many surrendered and the others beat a hasty retreat. 79 Volksgrenadier Division would continue to resist, but no longer had the strength for any further offensive operations.

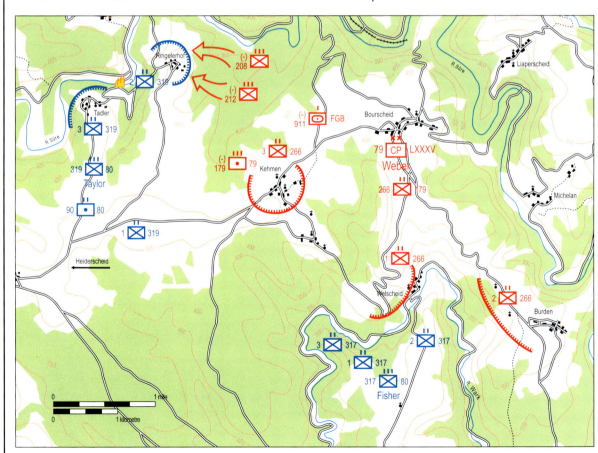

16/12/1944		17/12	18-19/12	20/12	21/12	22/12	23/12	24/12		25/12	26/12	27/12	28-29/12	30/12	31/12	1/1
pages 28-37,63-66,69-72		67-68		38-39		40-42	45-46,80-81	43-44,		82-83		84-85		49-50		

LXXXV KORPS' BATTLES
14 Fallschirm Regiment

Villers-la-Bonne-Eau – December 30–January 1

While 79 Volksgrenadier Division was launching its final assault against Ringelerhof on December 30, over to the northwest 14 Fallschirm Regiment, temporarily reassigned to Generalleutnant Karl Decker's XXXIX Panzer Korps of Fifth Panzer Armee, was also on the offensive. Heeresgruppe B commander Walter Model, still under pressure from Hitler to capture Bastogne, had carefully planned what was actually to prove the last major counter-attack of the whole Ardennes operation, using two Korps in a pincer operation designed once again to isolate the town from the outside world. 14 Fallschirm Regiment therefore dutifully took up station on the left flank of XXXIX Korps in the Lutrebois–Villers-la-Bonne-Eau–Harlange sector southeast of Bastogne, alongside what remained of the once proud 1 SS-Panzer Division in the centre, the similarly depleted Kampfgruppe '901' from Panzer 'Lehr', and the newly arrived 167 Volksgrenadier Division on the right.

While they attacked from the east, a simultaneous assault was launched from the northwest by XLVII Panzer Korps, the intention being that the two forces would join hands at or near Assenois. To support the attacking forces, Model brought forward 401 and 766 Volks-Artillerie Korps, by then totalling 321 guns and howitzers; plus 15 and 18 Volks-Werfer Brigaden with 306 Nebelwerfers. The big problem was that all, as usual, were short of ammunition and, in fact, the XLVII Korps assault spearheaded by the Führer Begleit Brigade never really got off its start line. Initial progress in the Harlange sector seemed, however, more promising.

The forces immediately facing Decker's Korps were the understrength 134th Infantry Regiment, 35th Infantry Division, around Lutrebois, and the 137th Regiment around Villers-la-Bonne-Eau, with Companies K and L actually in the village itself. To their south, and only marginally involved in the battle, was the 35th Division's 320th Regiment. (The battle for Lutrebois is covered in the companion volume.) The attack began at 0445 hrs on December 30 with infantry closely following the Leibstandarte's Panzers. At Villers-la-Bonne-Eau, 14 Fallschirm Regiment's leading companies were partnered apparently (different accounts are confusing) by seven Tiger IIs

The debris of battle. Wrecked American and German vehicles litter the landscape outside Villers-la-Bonne-Eau on New Year's Eve, marking the end of Hitler's ambitions on the Western Front.
(U.S. Signal Corps)

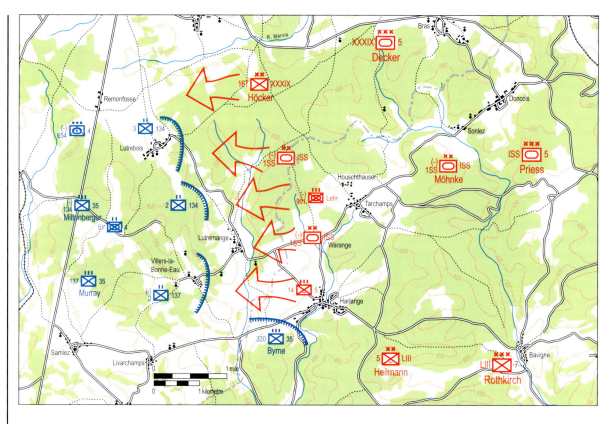

XXXIX Korps assault southeast of Bastogne achieved a small amount of local success at Lutrebois and Villers-la-Bonne-Eau but failed to dent the lines of the U.S. 35th Infantry Division significantly.

from the Leibstandarte's attached 501 schwere SS-Panzer Abteilung. The tanks' 8.8cm guns pulverised the stone walls of the houses which sheltered Companies K and L, and the Fallschirmjäger closed in, using flame-throwers to complete the job. The GIs managed to get out one last message at 0845 hrs calling for artillery support, then their radio went dead and the survivors surrendered. The Fallschirmjäger had done their work well, and out of 169 men in the two American companies, only one managed eventually to return to friendly lines.

On New Year's Eve, the American 35th Division commander, Major-General Paul Baade, still hoped the two companies of the 137th were managing to hold out and, in concert with a counter-attack by the remainder of the 134th (which had lost one of its own companies in Lutrebois), the balance of the 137th converged on Villers-la-Bonne-Eau on January

1. They were supported by troopers from the 6th Cavalry Squadron, fighting as infantry, and the reserve 1st Battalion of the 320th Infantry Regiment. Even so, and given their enormous artillery superiority, it took ten days to recapture the village and drive 14 Fallschirm Regiment into retreat. It was, according to the American regiment's own history, 'the roughest battle ever fought … ten days of bloodletting and frustration'. The greatest irony is that afterwards, the CO of 1 SS-Panzer Division tried to convene a Nazi field martial to convict 14 Fallschirm Regiment's officers of cowardice and negligence!

To conclude this section briefly, 15 Fallschirm Regiment on the 14th's left had not been involved in the December 30 offensive, but it did prove its mettle during the American counter-attack. At Fuhrman Farm, in front of Harlange, it managed to fight the remaining two battalions of the American 320th Regiment to a standstill on January 1. Next day, Model requested permission to pull 5 Fallschirm Division back east, but Hitler still refused. The survivors were thus amongst the last troops to make it back behind the river Our.

16/12/1944	17/12	18-19/12	20/12	21/12	22/12	23/12	24/12	25/12	26/12	27/12	28-29/12	30/12	31/12	1/1
pages 28-37,63-66,69-72	67-68		38-39		40-42	45-46,80-81	43-44,47-48	82-83		84-85				

SEVENTH ARMEE

LXXX KORPS

Discounting LIII Korps, which at the start of 'Herbstnebel' merely consisted of two battalions guarding the twelve-mile (20km) stretch of West Wall behind the river Sauer/Saar between Seventh and First Armees, General der Infanterie Dr Franz Beyer's LXXX Korps formed the left wing of Heeresgruppe B for the new offensive. Severely lacking in manpower and matériel, the Korps was only assigned limited objectives and was fortunate in that the opposing American forces were also weak on December 16.

Beyer moved his divisions into place over the two nights preceding Null-Tag, with Generalmajor Kurt Möhring's 276 Volksgrenadier Division on the right between Wallendorf and Bollendorf occupying fox-holes already dug by the men of 352 Volksgrenadier Division, which had been guarding this stretch of the river Sauer before re-assembling to the north as part of LXXXV Korps. (An unforeseen bonus from this reshuffle was that American suspicions of an impending attack were lulled when patrols found the German foxholes deserted.) All that immediately

---

LXXX KORPS
General der Infanterie Franz Beyer
Stab

---

212 Volksgrenadier Division (Sensfuss)
276 Volksgrenadier Division (Möhring/Dempwolff)
 (to LIII Korps January 18)
340 Volksgrenadier Division (Tolsdorff)
 (from Fifteenth Armee December 26)
408 Volks-Artillerie Korps
8 Volks-Werfer Brigade

---

opposed Möhring was the U.S. 9th Armored Division's 60th Armored Infantry Battalion, giving his leading two regiments something like a six to one advantage. Behind this battalion, though, lay the remainder of 9th Armored's Combat Command A.

On Möhring's left from Bollendorf, past Echternach, to Edingen and Ralingen, was stationed Generalleutnant Franz Sensfuss' 212 Volksgrenadier

The confluence of the rivers Our and Sauer at Wallendorf, the most northerly crossing point chosen for LXXX Korps. American shelling from positions on the high ground behind Haller was so intense here that bridge-building for 276 Volksgrenadier Division had to be abandoned and a new site chosen at Bollendorf.
(U.S. Signal Corps)

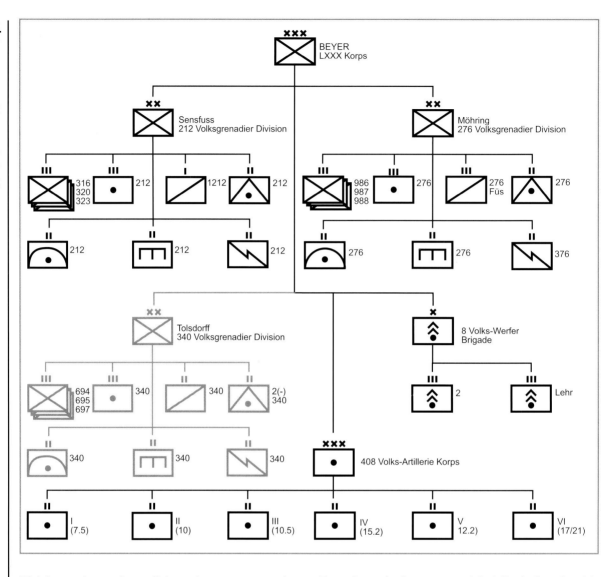

Division, whose immediate adversary was the 12th Regiment of the 4th Infantry Division, strung out in company-size pickets in villages on the west bank of the Sauer from Berdorf to Mompach. Unlike the men of the 9th Armored Division, who were so far untried in battle, these were seasoned veterans who had stormed 'Utah' beach on D-Day and were not just going to be pushed aside six months later. General

---

LXXX KORPS RESERVE

---

408 Volks-Artillerie Korps
(As Armee Reserve data)

8 Volks-Werfer Brigade
2 & Lehr Werfer Regimenten
(As Armee Reserve data)

Franz Beyer had encountered their like before, but this time he was fighting with one hand metaphorically tied behind his back.

As in the case of LXXXV Korps' CO, Baptist Kniess, Beyer had been a staff officer during the early campaigns of the war and did not receive his first independent field command until the same year, 1942. He then, with the rank of Generalmajor, took the Austrian 331 Infanterie Division into its first action on the central and then the northern sectors of the Russian front. The division was virtually destroyed in the spring of 1943 and was – unusually – withdrawn from the line to be rebuilt, at which point Beyer, now a Generalleutnant, took over the uniquely named (44) Reichsgrenadier Division 'Hoch und Deutschmeister'. This was another Austrian division (Beyer himself was Silesian) which had been formed after the destruction of the original 44 Infanterie Division at Stalingrad.

Beyer led it with panache in Italy during the retreat from Rome to the 'Gothic Line' before, with promotion to General der Infanterie, he took over LXXX Korps in General der Panzertruppen Otto von Knobelsdorff's First Armee on the Biscay coast, establishing his headquarters in Poitiers. (The Korps itself had originally been formed in 1939 as 'Grenzkommando I' in Poland, became XXXI Korps Kommando in Denmark in 1940 and was renumbered in 1942.)

Following the Allied breakout from Normandy and the invasion of southern France in August, First Armee was pulled back to join up with Friedrich Wiess' Nineteenth Armee in Lorraine, losing thousands of men from its low grade reserve divisions as deserters in the process. (It must be remembered that even this late in the war many Frenchmen in Vichy were still staunch Pétainists who sympathised with the German cause.) In October, Beyer and his staff were reassigned to Brandenberger's Seventh Armee and at the beginning of December learned of their role in the forthcoming Ardennes offensive.

LXXX Korps had roughly the same strength, on paper, as Kniess' LXXXV Korps on its right flank, with two Volksgrenadier divisions, 212 and 276. Of these, Brandenberger rated Franz Sensfuss' 212th his best division, and for this reason withheld its 316th Regiment as part of Seventh Armee Reserve, denying its use to Beyer until after Patton's counter-attack had begun. Nor did Beyer have any armour to support his initial assault apart from four or five StuGs in Sensfuss' division, although the four further assault guns allocated to Möhring's 276 Volksgrenadier Division did finally arrive from Milowitz on December 19. Moreover, the supporting 408 Volks-Artillerie Korps, like all except two in the Ardennes (388 and 766 with Sixth and Fifth Panzer Armees respectively), was lacking the sixth battalion with its heavy 17cm guns and 21cm mortars.

Unlike the men in LXXXV Korps, who had to force crossings of both the Our and Clerf, Beyer's troops just had one river to cross, the Sauer. However, south of its confluence with the Our at Wallendorf, the Sauer's course is winding and steep-banked; moreover, at this time of year, swollen by rain and snow, it is very fast-flowing, which caused problems both for the assault companies and the bridging engineers. The Korps' attack was further rendered difficult because of the American artillery batteries – with their seemingly inexhaustible supplies of ammunition – emplaced on the heights southwest of Beaufort and Echternach. This was why Model had placed so much emphasis on their removal in his operational orders to Brandenberger. A final complicating factor for Beyer was that, once across the Sauer, his divisions were effectively split by the deep gorge of the Schwarz Ernst, which flows through Müllerthal and in between Beaufort and Berdorf to join the Sauer between Dillingen and Bollendorf. This, Beyer feared, could also provide a natural route for an American counter-attack, which would drive a wedge through his Korps' centre. It was only belatedly that he realised the corollary was also true, and successfully released the third of 276 Volksgrenadier Division's regiments to penetrate deep behind American lines as far as Müllerthal on the second day of the offensive.

The Korps' attack began inauspiciously, because engineers had to abandon their attempt to build a bridge at Wallendorf thanks to the American artillery fire and start again at Bollendorf. The new bridge was not completed until December 20, therefore Beyer's infantry had to operate without artillery support to begin with, and at the end of the first day he was not pleased with progress, particularly by Möhring's 276 Volksgrenadier Division. Heavy fog had badly hampered the assault companies' progress, although

The Schwarz Ernst gorge gave speedy westward access to Möhring's reserve 987 Regiment on December 17. Müllerthal was captured unopposed, outflanking both the 60th Armored Infantry Battalion and the 4th Infantry Regiment, and the grenadiers threw back several American counter-attacks.
(U.S. Army Air Force)

Although mist and fog frequently gave cover for operations by both sides during the battle, attacks in broad daylight needed smokescreens. Here, American white phosphorous shells burst amongst 212 Volksgrenadier Division positions at Michelshof during Patton's counter-attack. (U.S. Signal Corps)

it also concealed them from the enemy, enabling them to cut off several American pickets and occupy Bigelbach. Similarly, north of Echternach, 212 Volksgrenadier Division's men reached Berdorf before the Americans realised an offensive was in progress. Soon, however, the CO of the U.S. 4th Infantry Division, Major-General Raymond Barton, discovered that Echternach, Lauterborn and Dickweiler were also under attack.

The situation improved slightly on the 17th, with 276 Volksgrenadier Division's capture of Müllerthal and Beaufort, cutting off three companies of 9th Armored's 60th Infantry Battalion and forcing the Americans to withdraw their artillery from the high ground behind Haller. An American counter-attack to rescue the isolated companies on December 18 fell into an ambush and failed disastrously (see also OOB 9). To the south, Berdorf and Lauterborn remained in American hands, as did Echternach itself and the villages of Dickweiler and Osweiler. Even though Sensfuss' men captured Scheidgen, threatening Consdorf further west, neither of Beyer's divisions was anywhere near achieving its initial objectives.

The situation began to deteriorate on December 18 with the arrival of CCB from 10th Armored Division which was split into three task forces to counter-attack at Berdorf, Müllerthal and towards Echternach along the Scheidgen road. The Americans were able to recapture Scheidgen easily because Sensfuss had moved his men south to exploit the gap in the American lines west of Herborn, and reached Mons Lellingen, deepening the dent in the 12th Infantry Regiment's centre. Other than this, however, 10th Armored's first forays proved inconclusive.

The struggle continued around the same villages over the next two days but, although Sensfuss' men finally captured Echternach late on December 20, the attack toward Christnach by 276 Volksgrenadier Division was a disaster. This marked the end of LXXX Korps' offensive operations and Beyer, having fallen far short of achieving most of his objectives, put his men on the defensive. This was just as well. When XII Corps from Patton's Third Army counter-attacked in force, principally with the 5th Infantry Division, Beyer's two depleted divisions were unable to put up an effective resistance. Even when Brandenberger released 316 Volksgrenadier Regiment from Armee Reserve, it was a mere drop in the ocean. The Korps was then assigned to Oberst Theodore Tolsdorff's 340 Volksgrenadier Division but when it finally arrived it was so depleted as to be of no practical value at all.

The LXXX Korps' zone of operation to the northeast of Luxembourg City is characterised by some of the most rugged terrain in the Ardennes, which obviously helped the defenders more than the attackers. In the south, 212 Volksgrenadier Division's assault reached as far west as Scheidgen but the stubborn American resistance in Echternach itself and the villages of Osweiler and Dickweiler tied up a large part of the division's strength – and it had only two regiments in the line. In the northern sector, 276 Volksgrenadier Division captured Müllerthal and Beaufort, surrounding the U.S. 60th Armored Infantry Battalion and forcing the Americans to withdraw the troublesome artillery batteries from behind Haller, but the division lacked the strength for its subsequent attacks towards Medernach and Christnach to succeed.

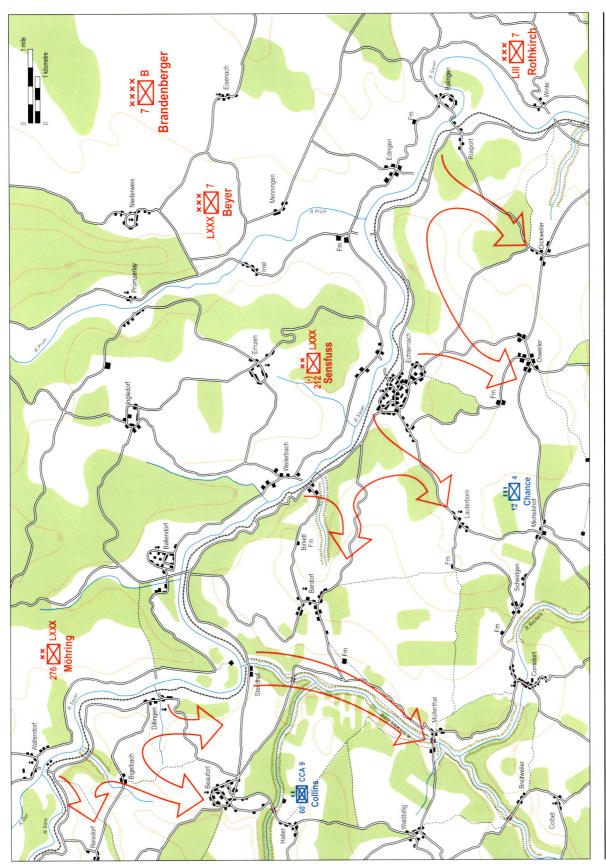

Seventh Armee – LXXX Korps

212 Volksgrenadier Division

Considered by Brandenberger to be by far the best division in Seventh Armee at the start of the offensive, Franz Sensfuss' 212 Volksgrenadier Division formed the southern pivot of the whole operation. Its orders were to take out the U.S. 4th Infantry Division's 12th Regiment's supporting artillery positions around Herborn and Mompach in the bend of the Sauer below Echternach; to establish a blocking line west of Wasserbilig and, if conditions were favourable, to advance as far as Junglinster, the American regimental headquarters (and home of Radio Luxembourg's powerful transmitter).

The terrain across which the division had to advance, 'Suisse Luxembourgoise', resembles indeed a miniature Alpine landscape, being almost vertical in places rather like Luxembourg City itself. These conditions obviously worked in the defenders' favour, and no one from von Rundstedt and Model down thought for a moment that Sensfuss' grenadiers would get anywhere near Junglinster except through freak chance, but the attempt – threatening the American 12th Army Group HQ itself in the capital – was bound to provoke a swift response. This would deny the Allies use of at least some of the reserves which they could otherwise have diverted to the main battlefield further north. It was, so to speak, 212 Volksgrenadier Division's task to wave the matador's cape, and try to avoid being gored by the bull.

Taking chances was nothing new to the veterans in Sensfuss' ranks, although it was to their commander, a fortress engineer by training and experience now in his first field command. The division itself dated back pre-war and was predominantly Bavarian, with its home station in München. In September 1939 it had been keeping a watching brief on the Maginot Line and took no part in the Polish campaign. In June 1940 it was still in the same place behind the river Saar, as a component in Feldmarschall Wilhelm von Leeb's Heeresgruppe C, but did participate in the 'demonstration' against the vaunted French defences which actually broke through at Bitche and resulted in the fall of Strasbourg – just as Hitler obviously hoped it would again in 1944 when he conceived operation 'Nordwind'.

After a brief spell of occupation duty, the division was withdrawn to Germany to be reorganised. Its older

212 VOLKSGRENADIER DIVISION
Generalleutnant Franz Sensfuss
Stabs Kompanie

316 Volksgrenadier Regiment (in Armee Reserve)
320 Volksgrenadier Regiment
423 Volksgrenadier Regiment
212 Füsilier Bataillon
212 Volks-Artillerie Regiment
1212 Aufklärungs Kompanie (Fahrrad)
212 Panzerjäger Abteilung (mot)
212 Flak Abteilung
212 Pionier Bataillon
212 Nachrichten Abteilung
1212 Nachschub Truppe
1212 Werkstatt Truppe
1212 Verwaltungs Truppe
1212 Sanitäts Truppe

personnel were transferred to other, static, formations and the 212th received younger replacements. They were still undergoing training in the summer of 1941 and the division took no part in operation 'Barbarossa' but was assigned to Heeresgruppe Mitte in December. It acquitted itself well during the Soviet winter counter-offensive either side of Moscow and was still in surprisingly good shape in the spring of 1942 when it was reassigned to Generaloberst Gerhardt Lindemann's Eighteenth Armee in Heeresgruppe Nord. Hitler had abandoned Moscow as an immediate goal and, dissatisfied with von Leeb's inability to take Leningrad, had replaced him by Generaloberst Georg von Küchler and ordered that the stubborn city 'be wiped off the face of the earth'.

The Russians, of course, had different ideas and assembled three armies (2nd Shock, 8th and 54th) in General K. A. Meretskov's Volkhov Front to attack south of Lake Ladoga and break through to the defenders of the besieged city. The assault, centred on the town of Sinyavino, began on August 24 and lasted a month before it was called off. Generalleutnant Theodore Endres' 212 Infanterie Division was heavily engaged throughout and incurred proportionate casualties. (Altogether, some 60,000 Germans lost their lives during this period.)

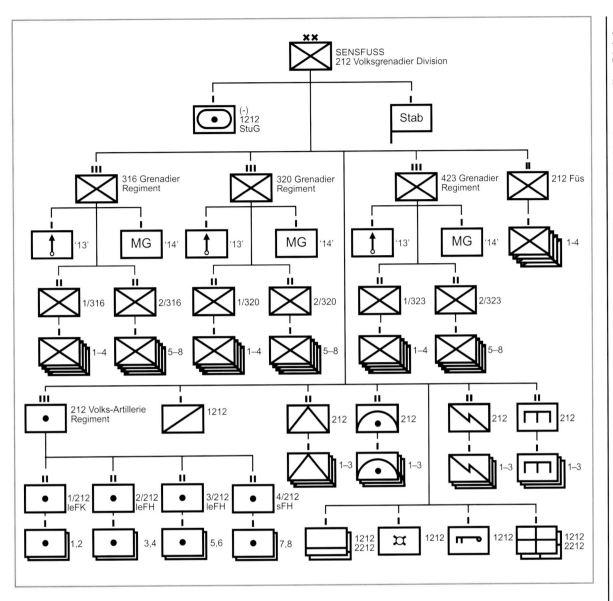

As 1942 drew to a close, all eyes were focused on the drama being played out at Stalingrad, and Eleventh Armee was transferred from Heeresgruppe Nord to help in the fighting further south. Soviet intelligence detected this weakening of the German defences east of Leningrad, and Meretskov launched a second offensive south of Lake Ladoga on January 12 1943. Within six days Volkhov Front had broken through to lift the siege, although German artillery continued to pound the city. 212 Infanterie Division again suffered heavily but was kept in the line and now had a reprieve because the Russians made no further major aggressive moves in its sector that year.

The next Soviet offensive began on January 14 1944 and by the beginning of March Eighteenth Armee had been driven back to the Estonian border, where a solid line of defence had been built using the natural barrier of Lake Peipus. Even this proved inadequate when the Red Army renewed its assault at the beginning of July, and 212 Infanterie Division (now commanded by Generalmajor Dr Karl Koske) was forced to retreat through Estonia and into Lithuania where it was finally shattered in August.

The survivors formed the nucleus of a new 212 Volksgrenadier Division, which officially came into being on September 17 after absorbing 578 Volksgrenadier Division, which was then assembling at Schieratz in Poland. As in the case of the original division, most of its personnel were Bavarian and, unlike many in other Volksgrenadier divisions, were largely young – some, in fact, only seventeen. Moved west at the beginning of November, the division took its place on Seventh Armee's left, behind the Sauer at Echternach. Its rifle regiments were at full strength and morale was high, but it had only four or five StuGs to support the assault in December and its Aufklärungs Abteilung consisted of a single bicycle company! Moreover, it had only two of its rifle regiments for the attack, 320 and 423, because Brandenberger withheld 316 Regiment in Armee Reserve and did not release it back to Sensfuss until it was too late to be of any help.

The division's assault began before dawn, 423 Regiment leading the way on the right, west of Echternach, heading towards Berdorf, and 320 Regiment on the left heading towards Dickweiler and Osweiler, where the defending American companies stubbornly refused to be dislodged and were very quickly reinforced. In fact, II/320 Regiment suffered so badly in its attacks on Dickweiler that it ceased to be an effective tactical fighting force for the rest of the battle. The assault companies were screened by a thick mist as they paddled across the Sauer while engineers began work on a bridge for the StuGs and artillery at Edingen. The first phase of the attack went extremely smoothly and Sensfuss' grenadiers were well behind the American lines before the commander of the U.S. 4th Infantry Division, Major-General Raymond Barton, received the first report of their presence at 1015 hrs. By this time, 423 Regiment had overrun the forward American outposts, cut the Echternach–Junglinster road and reached Berdorf and Lauterborn. 320 Regiment, unable to cross as planned at Echternach because of the swift river current,

Taken earlier in the year, this aerial reconnaissance photo shows the tiny village of Berdorf, which in December was defended against Franz Sensfuss' 423 Regiment by F Company of the 12th Infantry Regiment's 2nd Battalion. (U.S. Army Air Force)

crossed at Edingen instead but encountered stiff opposition in Echternach itself, as well as in the villages of Dickweiler and Osweiler.

On December 17, Combat Command A of 10th Armored Division from Patton's Third Army began moving into position for a counter-attack on the 18th. The command was split into three task forces, two of which headed for Berdorf and Lauterborn where 423 Regiment put up such a fight that they had to withdraw. The third task force reached Echternach and offered to cover the withdrawal of the rifle company still defending the town, but the senior officer there refused, saying he was under orders to make 'no retrograde movement', and the tanks withdrew.

The American garrison held out throughout the 19th, but on the 20th Sensfuss personally led a fresh assault by 212 Füsilier Bataillon, supported by a single StuG, which finally forced the surviving 132 defenders in Echternach to surrender. Sensfuss himself was slightly wounded in the attack but continued in command. On the same day, I Bataillon of 423 Regiment launched its own counter-attack at Berdorf, which forced the 10th Armored Division task force to evacuate the bitterly contested little village. This, however, was the high tide of 212 Volksgrenadier Division's advance.

When Patton threw XII Corps into the counter-attack, Sensfuss gradually had to give up his hard-won gains and by the end of January 1945 the division had lost over 4,000 men. Although the division's rifle companies were reduced to a strength of a mere 25 to 30 men, they refused to give up even when Patton's troops smashed through the West Wall in February. Finally reduced to a small kampfgruppe, the division continued to resist until the end of hostilities, though, not surrendering, near Baumholder in Bavaria, until May.

276 Volksgrenadier Division

Generalmajor Kurt Möhring's 276 Volksgrenadier Division formed the right flank of LXXX Korps and moved up to its start line east of the Sauer during the two nights preceding December 16. The division was in poor shape so was only given the limited objective of Bissen, just west of the river Alzette, but did not even get half that far.

An original 276 Infanterie Division began forming in June 1940 but never saw action and was disbanded after the fall of France. A second was activated at Hannover in November and, commanded by Generalleutnant Kurt Badinski, at the time of D-Day was stationed at Bayonne. Even then, it was far from being an elite formation, most of its personnel being middle-aged and drawn from reserved occupations, such as mining. It was not therefore rushed to Normandy but arrived at the beginning of July, holding the sector formerly occupied by 12 SS-Panzer Division for a month before being almost completely destroyed in the Falaise pocket.

Like so many others, it was reconstituted as a Volksgrenadier division in September, absorbing the partially formed 580 Volksgrenadier Division then in Poland. Many of its men were still convalescing from wounds and when Möhring assumed command he considered few of them fit for combat, and their morale low. Nevertheless, the division was at almost full strength although it had no StuGs when, on November 15, it entrained for the west and assembled near Bitburg.

Brandenberger's orders called for Möhring's division to capture the high ground west of the Sauer around Beaufort and Eppeldorf, take out the troublesome American artillery positions at Haller and then extend the line further west to protect 352 Volksgrenadier Division's left flank. The attack began in thick fog before dawn on December 16 following a short barrage by the Korps' artillery and rocket projectors. The fog concealed the rubber assault boats and Möhring's grenadiers were able to make some progress, infiltrating behind the American outposts using the steep-sided gullies leading west from the Sauer. However, the division's main bridging point at Wallendorf had already been pinpointed by the Americans and their artillery fire was so accurate and intense that the engineers had to abandon the attempt

and start again at Bollendorf.

At the end of the first day the division was still far short of achieving its initial objectives. It had taken some largely uncontested ground, but had failed to secure the heights west of the Sauer, and the American guns at Haller were still firing. Brandenberger ordered Möhring in no uncertain terms to press on with the attack during the night, and began thinking urgently about replacing him. The dressing-down worked, and Möhring's 986 and 988 Regiments achieved a great deal more on the 17th. By daybreak, they had cut off the three rifle companies of the 60th Armored Infantry Regiment from their headquarters in Beaufort, and on the division's left the reserve 987 Regiment advanced unopposed up the Schwarz Ernst gorge to capture Müllerthal.

Here, they easily repulsed a half-hearted counter-attack. On the right flank, the 986th was less lucky because, although they captured Eppeldorf, this time an American counter-attack was a success. The greatest gain was achieved by the 988th just after darkness fell when it infiltrated Beaufort itself, forcing the 60th Armored's CO, Lieutenant-Colonel Kenneth Collins, to withdraw his headquarters to Savelborn. This put the 3rd Armored Field Artillery Battalion at Haller under threat and the guns also withdrew during

---

276 VOLKSGRENADIER DIVISION

Generalmajor Kurt Möhring/
Oberst Hugo Dempwolff

Stabs Kompanie

---

986 Volksgrenadier Regiment
987 Volksgrenadier Regiment
988 Volksgrenadier Regiment
276 Volks-Artillerie Regiment
276 Füsilier Grenadier Bataillon
276 Panzerjäger Abteilung
276 Flak Abteilung
276 Pionier Bataillon
276 Nachrichten Abteilung
1276 Nachschub Truppe
1276 Werkstatt Truppe
1276 Verwaltungs Truppe
1276 Sanitäts Truppe

the night, leaving Möhring's pioniere to work in peace.

Despite these small successes on December 17, Brandenberger had already decided that someone more decisive was needed in charge of the 267th, and had issued orders that Möhring should be replaced by his deputy, Oberst Hugo Dempwolff. However, that same evening Möhring's car was caught in a burst of machine-gun fire while he was travelling from Beaufort to Müllerthal and he was killed. Before this, though, he had already issued his own orders for December 18, which were for an attack towards Medernach from the woods east of the Ermsdorf–Savelborn road. At the same time, the CO of 9th Armored Division's CCA, Colonel Thomas Harrold, had planned a further relief column to try to extricate his three infantry companies still trapped on the banks of the Sauer. The relief force was ambushed and almost annihilated, but this was

virtually 276 Volksgrenadier Division's last throw.

The new CO, Dempwolff, spent December 19 reorganising his forces and brought his artillery, plus the four StuGs which had finally arrived, across the Sauer and Our over 212 and 352 Volksgrenadier Divisions' bridges at Weilerbach and Gentingen. He attacked towards Christnach on the 20th and succeeded in capturing Waldbillig, but now facing the whole of the rest of CCA/9th, lost the precious StuGs, and that, in effect, was that. After being transferred to von Rothkirch's LIII Korps, the 276th lost so many men during the Allied counter-offensive that the survivors were attached to 79 Volksgrenadier Division. Retreating towards the Rhein in March, now commanded by Oberst Werner Wagner, the 'division' was reduced to about 400 men when it was finally smashed south of Remagen.

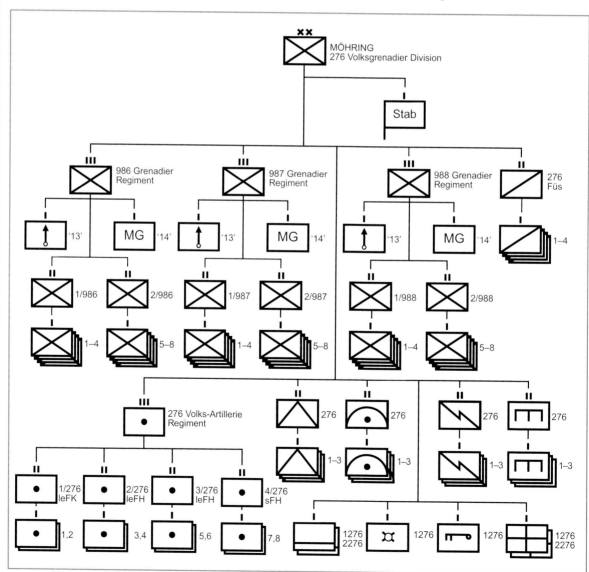

340 Volksgrenadier Division

Being stranded without fuel was a common ailment amongst all the German forces assembled for 'Herbstnebel', or drawn later into the struggle. The lack of Luftwaffe support was another common and valid complaint. Oberst Theodor Tolsdorff, though, the recently appointed commander of 340 Volksgrenadier Division, had more than usual grounds to protest, for not only was his force's appearance on the battlefield delayed for the first reason, but it also then suffered the ignomiy of being bombed by its own air force.

Commanded by Generalleutnant Friedrich von Neumann, the original 340 Infanterie Division was formed in the East Prussian capital, Königsberg, in January 1941 and, after a brief posting to Hamburg, was stationed in the Pas de Calais. A year later, now commanded by Generalleutnant Wilhelm Butze, it entrained for less cosy billets in Russia where it joined Heeresgruppe Süd. The division was heavily engaged during the Soviet winter counter-offensive of 1942–43 and at Kharkov in the spring, and suffered further casualties during the retreat through the Ukraine following the battle of Kursk. By February 1944 its rifle regiments were at battalion strength and it had only half its artillery pieces left. In June the division was finally encircled near Lvov and was practically destroyed.

The few men who escaped formed the veteran cadre for a new 340 Volksgrenadier Division in September. This absorbed the partially formed 572 Grenadier Division then assembling in the Stettin region, but was still understrength when it was committed to battle east of Aachen in November. Its commander, Oberst Theodor Tolsdoff, came from the original division's home town, Königsberg, and, at the age of 35, had already won the Knights Cross with Oakleaves and Swords.

At the beginning of operation 'Herbstnebel' the division formed part of General der Infanterie Gustav-Adolf von Zangen's Fifteenth Armee, but on December 26 it was ordered south and, in the first place, joined not LXXX Korps but I SS-Panzer Korps which had itself been transferred from Sixth to Fifth Panzer Armee. The division was still trudging south, bedevilled by the usual fuel shortages and traffic jams, when it was assigned alongside 9 and 12 SS-Panzer

---

340 VOLKSGRENADIER DIVISION
Oberst Theodor Tolsdorff
Stabs Kompanie

694 Volksgrenadier Regiment
695 Volksgrenadier Regiment
696 Volksgrenadier Regiment
340 Volks-Artillerie Regiment
340 Aufklärungs Abteilung (Fahrrad)
340 Panzerjäger Abteilung (-)
340 Flak Abteilung (?)
340 Pionier Bataillon
340 Nachrichten Abteilung
1340 Nachschub Truppe
1340 Werkstatt Truppe
1340 Verwaltungs Truppe
1340 Sanitäts Truppe

Divisions to 'Kampfraum Bastogne' on January 1 1945. Having already suffered heavily during the earlier fighting at Aachen, the division's rifle battalions were each down to a strength of about 150 men and when it was committed to the attack northeast of Bastogne on January 2 its artillery was still en route, as was that of 12 SS-Panzer Division.

The Americans pre-empted I SS-Panzer Korps' attack by launching their own with CCA of 6th Armored Division heading out of Bastogne toward Wardin and CCB toward Mageret. Toldsdorff's kampfgruppe – no longer a division except in name – began its assault at 1400 hrs with 12 SS-Panzer Division on its right and 9 SS-Panzer behind it, and a detachment of the 340th actually managed to break into Mageret, scene of an earlier victory for 2 Panzer Division during its drive to the Meuse.

The Luftwaffe now put in an appearance. German planes had been enthusiastically bombing Bastogne for the previous couple of days instead of more usefully supporting XLVII and XXXIX Korps' attacks at Sibret and Lutrebois. Now the aircraft reappeared and bombed Mageret, causing more casualties amongst the Volksgrenadiers than the opposing 68th Tank Battalion.

Tolsdorff's success was brief and within a couple of hours the American tanks had repossessed Mageret,

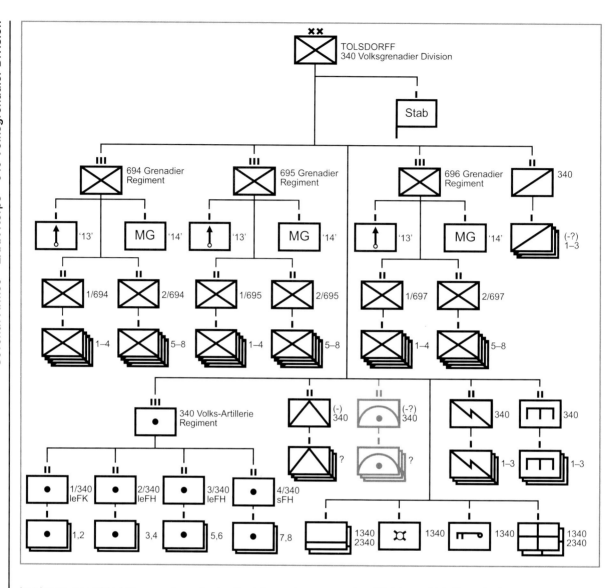

but he reassembled his men for a fresh attack toward Bizory on January 3, this time supported by the Jagdpanzer IVs of 12 SS-Panzerjäger Abteilung. Here they ran up against the U.S. 501st Parachute Infantry Regiment and 'it soon transpired', reported Korps' commander Hermann Priess afterwards, 'that the Volksgrenadiers' strength, one weak regiment, was insufficient for the wooded area in which they were fighting. In spite of this, however, they succeeded by evening in gaining about half a kilometre of ground.'

The fighting continued until January 6 and caused even Patton some concern because 6th Armored Division was forced to retreat for the first time in its history. However, Model was obliged to call the attack off because of the mounting pressure from Hodges' U.S. First Army further north, and the survivors of 340 Volksgrenadier Division passed to Beyer's LXXX Korps in Seventh Armee, replacing 276 Volks-

grenadier Division which Brandenberger had by now reassigned to LIII Korps.

The Korps itself was in full retreat by this time and Tolsdorff's tiny command could not hope to affect the outcome. It was relentlessly pushed back towards the southeast, behind the river Sauer, and in February made contact with troops of Generalmajor Karl Brizelmayr's 19 Volksgrenadier Division on the right flank of SS-Gruppenführer Max Simon's XIII SS-Korps which had been repulsed by the U.S. 44th Infantry Division around Sarreguemines during operation 'Nordwind'. 340 Volksgrenadier Division was then re-assigned to Simon's Korps, retreating toward Koblenz 'in tiny remnants', according to the U.S. official history. The division was finally dissolved in March and its few survivors incorporated in 19 Volksgrenadier Division which did not, however, surrender in Bavaria until the end of hostilities.

LXXX KORPS' BATTLES
986 Volksgrenadier Regiment

Wallendorf/Savelborn – December 16–18

Having shortened its lines to allow 352 and 212 Volksgrenadier Divisions to move up to the rivers Our/Sauer on either flank, on the morning of December 16 Generalmajor Kurt Möhring's 276 Volksgrenadier Division was deployed between Wallendorf in the north and Bollendorf to the southeast. 986 Regiment was on the right, or northern, flank, with 988 Regiment on its left and 987 temporarily in reserve.

The attack by 986 Volksgrenadier Regiment did not begin smoothly. The Korps artillery fire had been directed principally at the town of Beaufort and the Americans' own artillery batteries at Haller and did no damage to the GIs on the high ground overlooking the river (Companies A and C of the 60th Armored Infantry Battalion from 9th Armored Division). There was considerable confusion as pioniere manhandled the unwieldy rubber assault craft down the steep eastern bank at Wallendorf and, although the early morning river mist concealed the crossings from the enemy, it also made navigation difficult once the men were on the thickly wooded western shore.

The first assault companies which got across at about 0630 hrs nevertheless made fairly quick progress, using the lie of the land to show them the direction they should be moving in, and II/986 on the right flank headed west between Reisdorf and Bigelbach, intending initially to reach the commanding high ground in front of Berens. They overran a squad of the American Company C but then, as daylight slowly emerged, came under heavy flanking fire from men of the 3rd Battalion, 109th Infantry Regiment, on the high ground north of the river Sûre. This temporarily forced them to go to ground within spitting distance of Reisdorf.

On the regiment's left flank, I/986 meanwhile had taken the village of Bigelbach unopposed but then itself came under flanking fire from Company C, 60th Armored Infantry Battalion, and inexplicably did not push on but contented itself with exchanging smallarms fire at long range. By this time, of course, the commander of the 60th, Lieutenant-Colonel Kenneth Collins, was all too well aware of the fact that not only was he under attack, but so were the 109th Regiment of 28th Infantry Division on his left and the 12th Regiment of 4th Infantry Division on his right. He therefore moved his reserve Company B forward to reinforce Companies A and C but, although they still had control of the heights overlooking the Sauer, both their flanks were open.

At the end of the day Seventh Armee commander General Brandenberger was highly dissatisfied with 986 Volksgrenadier Regiment's progress, and told General Möhring so in no uncertain terms. Even this early Brandenberger was already thinking about replacing Möhring by someone more energetic. On December 17, therefore, II/986 did move forward and briefly occupied Eppeldorf, but was then thrown out by a counter-attack by light tanks of the 89th Cavalry Reconnaissance Squadron. By this time Colonel Thomas Harrold, commander of CCA, 9th Armored Division, had been given overall control of the Beaufort sector, but was hampered in deploying his 19th Tank Battalion's M4s effectively because of the urgent appeals for help from the 109th and 12th Infantry Regiments on either flank. Moreover, a new threat had emerged since Möhring had released his reserve 987 Regiment, which had used the cover of the Schwarz Ernst gorge to penetrate deeply behind his lines as far as Müllerthal.

At the end of December 17 Colonel Collins was forced to withdraw his command post from Beaufort and also pull the 3rd Armored Field Artillery battalion back from Haller to Savelborn, in the centre of a new

16/12/1944		17/12	18-19/12	20/12	21/12	22/12	23/12	24/12	25/12	26/12	27/12	28-29/12	30/12	31/12	1/1
pages 28-37,65-66,69-72		67-68		38-39		40-42	45-46,80-81	43-44,47-48	82-83		84-85		49-50		

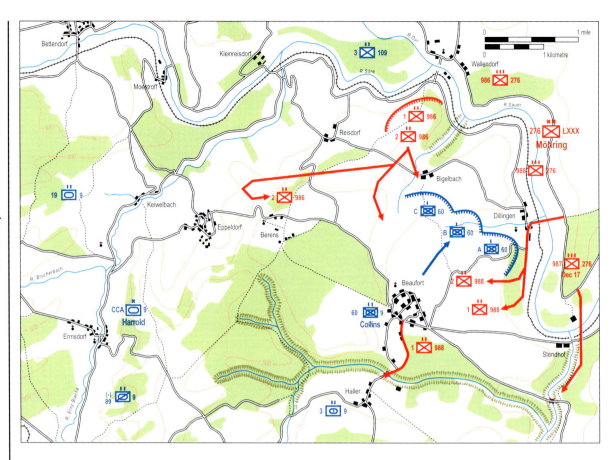

Although its initial progress was slow due to flanking fire from American troops north of the Sûre, 986 Volksgrenadier Regiment helped to encircle the 60th Armored Infantry Battalion and later successfully ambushed the task forces sent to its relief.

line of defence which Colonel Harrold was constructing between Ermsdorf and Waldbillig. However, the three companies of the 60th Armored Infantry Battalion were now completely cut off, with troops of both 986 and 988 Volksgrenadier Regiments behind them. Even so, Brandenberger was still displeased with 276 Volksgrenadier Division's progress, and issued orders for Möhring's dismissal. Whether the unfortunate General ever received them is unclear, because he was killed by a burst of machine-gun fire while travelling from Beaufort to Müllerthal that evening. However, he had already issued his own orders to 986 Regiment for December 18, which were to reap an unexpected dividend.

With the 60th Armored Infantry Battalion still cut off,

Colonel Harrold decided to mount a rescue operation – but all his command now consisted of was Company B of the 19th Tank Battalion, Company A of the 9th Armored Engineer Battalion, the I&R Platoon and one platoon each of light tanks and tank destroyers. He organised them into two task forces under Captain John Hall and Major Tommie Philbeck which set out towards Berens before dawn on the 18th. However, Möhring's last order had sent I/986 Volksgrenadier Regiment plus the regimental anti-tank company to attack across the Ermsdorf–Savelborn road towards Medernach, and this force had assembled during the night in the woods either side of the road to Berens. CCA/9th's I&R Platoon, reconnoitring the route, was cut to pieces. Captain Hall's task force moved unaware into the trap. His leading M5 was knocked out, blocking the road, and he himself was wounded. Then, when Major Philbeck arrived on the scene, 986 Regiment's Panzerfausts accounted for seven Shermans, forcing the survivors of both task forces to fall back to Savelborn.

16/12/1944	17/12	18-19/12	20/12	21/12	22/12	23/12	24/12	25/12	26/12	27/12	28-29/12	30/12	31/12	1/1
pages 28-37,65-66,69-72	67-68	38-39	40-42		45-46,80-81	43-44,47-48		82-83		84-85		49-50		

LXXX KORPS' BATTLES

988 Volksgrenadier Regiment

Dillingen/Beaufort – December 16–18

On 986 Volksgrenadier Regiment's left, 988 Volksgrenadier Regiment crossed the Sauer around Dillingen, heading towards Beaufort and the troublesome American artillery positions behind Haller. These guns were a top priority because their field of fire covered both 276 Volksgrenadier Division's bridging points at Dillingen and Wallendorf, and until they were removed none of the divisional artillery, nor its four Sturmgeschütze, could be brought across the river. Immediately in their path on the high ground in front of Beaufort overlooking Dillingen lay Company A of the American 60th Armored Infantry Battalion. Although this had a strong position, it had insufficient men to cover every gully and ravine running from the river up towards the heights through the dense pinewoods. By midday, therefore, large numbers of Volksgrenadiers had infiltrated through Company A's positions, as well as to both flanks.

The 60th Armored Infantry Battalion commander, Lieutenant-Colonel Kenneth Collins, had no choice but to release Company B from reserve to fill the gap in between Companies A and C. The new arrival had several skirmishes with parties of Volksgrenadiers pushing west, but reached its assigned position abreast the other two. Meanwhile, the 3rd Armored Field Artillery Battalion batteries at Haller continued to pound the bridging points and the river bank in front of the three companies of armoured infantry. In mid-afternoon, the U.S. 9th Armored Division commander, Major-General John Leonard, dipped into the small reserves he had in this sector to send the armoured cars of Troop A from the 89th Cavalry

Frequently published but still evocative portrait of a grenadier munching on a bar of chocolate. Even in winter the chicken wire on the helmet helped break up its silhouette. (U.S. Signal Corps)

Reconnaissance Squadron to guard the approach to Beaufort. As night fell, however, 988 Volksgrenadier Regiment had made no more significant progress than had 986 Regiment on its right beyond encircling the three American companies on the Sauer heights. These were well dug in and had so far prevented the regiment from making a co-ordinated attack. Instead, there were just several individual firefights up and down the line. Although the divisional artillery on the east bank of the Sauer gave what support it could, lack of ammunition – as throughout Seventh Armee – prevented this being effective.

December 17 brought more hope. Concerned over 276 Volksgrenadier Division's lack of progress, Brandenberger authorised Generalmajor Kurt Möhring to release 987 Regiment from reserve to attack on the division's left flank using the rocky defile of the Schwarz Ernst gorge to penetrate deeply behind the American lines. This forced Colonel Thomas Harrold, CO of 9th Armored's Combat Command A who that morning assumed control over the Beaufort sector, to divert resources to meet the new threat, easing

16/12/1944		17/12	18-19/12	20/12	21/12	22/12	23/12	24/12		25/12	26/12	27/12	28-29/12	30/12	31/12	1/1
pages 28-37,63-64,69-72		67-68		38-39		40-42	45-46,80-81	43-44,47-48		82-83		84-85		49-50		

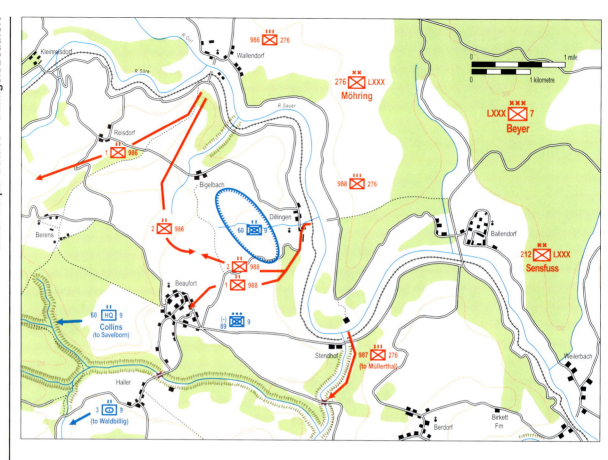

While 988 Volksgrenadier Regiment was able to penetrate the 60th Armored Infantry Battalion's lines and surround them, American artillery fire prevented any more significant advance until nightfall on December 17.

988 Regiment's task. Although Harrold dipped into his reserves to send half a dozen Greyhound armoured cars from Beaufort to try to break through to his three trapped companies, they were unable to drive the Volksgrenadiers from the woods. For their own part, the grenadiers had been unable to advance any further during daylight because as soon as they emerged from the pines they ran into a hailstorm of artillery fire as well as direct fire from three Headquarters Company M4s on the edge of Beaufort.

As darkness fell, however, small groups of grenadiers began cautiously emerging from their shelter and seeping into the streets of the town. They successfully overran a mortar platoon on its eastern edge and, picking up momentum as more and more

men arrived, were soon fighting house-to-house against those of the 60th Armored Infantry Battalion's Headquarters Company. The battalion commander, Colonel Collins, prudently ordered a withdrawal to the CCA assembly point at Savelborn, leaving Captain Victor Leiker's Troop A, 89th Cavalry Reconnaissance Squadron, as a rearguard. Leiker held on until 2030 hrs, by which time I/288 Volksgrenadier Regiment had control of the town and was pushing further west towards Waldbillig. Leiker lost 43 men and seven Greyhounds during this action.

On December 18, as we have seen, Colonel Harrold tried unsuccessfully to relieve the three armoured infantry companies who were now trapped deep behind 276 Volksgrenadier Division's lines. Meanwhile, the 3rd Armored Field Artillery Battalion had also been forced to pull back from Haller and Colonel Collins radioed the trapped companies to fight their way out west. Over the next three days the majority made it, but the battalion had lost 231 men and was now barely at company strength.

16/12/1944		17/12	18-19/12	20/12	21/12	22/12	23/12		24/12		25/12	26/12	27/12	28-29/12	30/12	31/12	1/1
pages 28-37,63-64,69-72		67-68		38-39		40-42	45-46,80-81		43-44,47-48		82-83		84-85		49-50		

LXXX KORPS' BATTLES

987 Volksgrenadier Regiment

Müllerthal – December 17–25

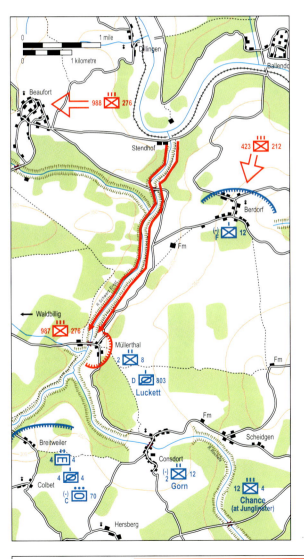

What is surprising to the historian, and equally surprised the Americans at the time, is that General Möhring made no attempt to exploit the natural avenue of the steep-walled Schwarz Ernst gorge right at the beginning of 276 Volksgrenadier Division's attack. This narrow river valley pointed like an arrow deep into American lines along the boundary of the 60th Armored Infantry Battalion on the north side and the 2nd Battalion of the 12th Infantry Regiment, 4th Infantry Division, to the south. However, spurred on by Brandenberger, Möhring released his reserve 987 Volksgrenadier Regiment on December 17 and, crossing at the loop in the Sauer below Dillingen, the leading battalion occupied Müllerthal late in the morning.

This posed a serious threat to both the 60th Armored and II/12th Battalion command posts in Beaufort and Consdorf, and obviously could not be ignored even though the Volksgrenadiers appeared content to proceed no further for the time being. The gorge is an attractive place in summer for tourists to stroll, but the snow and ice-covered rocks in the depths of winter are treacherous and it is possible the German battalion commander simply decided he had done enough for one day. Whatever, he gave the Americans a breathing space.

First on the scene to counter the threat came Troop B of the 89th Cavalry Reconnaissance Squadron plus four M18s of the 811th Tank Destroyer Battalion. Approaching Müllerthal from Waldbillig, the leading tank destroyer was hit by a Panzerfaust round, blocking the narrow road, and as the cavalry troopers tried to deploy, they were pinned down by accurate machine-gun and smallarms fire until nightfall. On the

Even though 987 Volksgrenadier Regiment made no serious attempt to break out from Müllerthal, their presence in the Schwarz Ernst gorge tied down a significant number of American tanks and infantry and caused them heavy casualties.

16/12/1944		17/12	18-19/12	20/12	21/12	22/12	23/12	24/12		25/12	26/12	27/12	28-29/12	30/12	31/12	1/1
pages 28-37,63-66,69-72				38-39		40-42	45-46,80-81	43-44,47-48		82-83		84-85		49-50		

other side of the gorge, the 4th Infantry Division commander, General Raymond Barton, had already sent the 4th Engineer Combat Battalion and 4th Reconnaissance Troop to the village of Breitweiler, and he now despatched a mixed force comprising the 2nd Battalion of the 8th Infantry Regiment and the reconnaissance company from the 803rd Tank Destroyer Battalion to block the exit from the gorge at Müllerthal. Later in the day the Americans received welcome reinforcement in the form of Brigadier-General Edwin Pilburn's Combat Command A, 10th Armored Division. Because of the approaching night, though, a counter-attack was postponed until December 18.

Early in the morning a mixed tank and infantry task force led by Lieutenant-Colonel Thomas Chamberlain set off for Müllerthal. The trail – it could scarcely be called a road – leading toward the village is steep sided and rugged, so the tanks had to advance in single file. As had happened to the tank destroyer sortie from the other side of the gorge the previous day, the counter-attack immediately stalled when a well-aimed shot from a Panzerfaust crippled the leading Sherman, forcing the others into a tortuous detour around it. The battalion from the 8th Infantry Regiment already in place tried to lend a hand but, although a few Volksgrenadiers were forced to vacate high-ground positions, the battle ended with nightfall.

December 19 was a great day for 987 Volksgrenadier Regiment and a disaster for the Americans. First, II/8th attempted to hook round Müllerthal from the left, but by this time engineers had completed a bridge at Dillingen and for once it was German artillery fire which broke up the attack with heavy casualties. Undeterred, the overall American commander on the spot, Colonel James Luckett, tried to hook around from the right, but again 276 Volksgrenadier Division's gunners were too accurate and Company E was all but wiped out. At this point General Barton called the whole operation off, ordered Chamberlain's task force back to Consdorf and just left Luckett's men in place to prevent a sortie out of the gorge.

The stalemate continued until Christmas Eve, after the Americans received further reinforcements in the shape of Major-General LeRoy Irwin's 5th Infantry Division, XII Corps. While launching two-pronged attacks towards Haller and Berdorf either side of the Schwarz Ernst, Irwin also decided to try his hand at

dislodging the stubborn Volksgrenadiers from Müllerthal. To this end he committed Colonel Worrell Roffe's 2nd Battalion, 2nd Infantry Regiment. Leading the way, Companies F and G immediately encountered exactly the same problems as Chamberlain's and Luckett's task forces. By this time of course the Volksgrenadiers were well dug-in in carefully selected and camouflaged positions with overlapping fields of fire. Ducking from tree to tree, the GIs could make no significant headway and suffered badly from ricochets off the rocks, the flattened 7.92mm rounds causing horrific wounds. On Christmas morning they had to fight their way back out to the lip of the gorge, and were then thrown into the battle for Berdorf.

It was now the turn of the unlucky Company A from the 1st Battalion, 11th Infantry Regiment, 5th Infantry Division, to try their luck from the other side of the gorge. Descending from the direction of Waldbillig, they came under such heavy fire that once again they were pinned down until darkness could cover their withdrawal. It was almost the last act, though, because with the Americans rapidly pushing back 276 Volksgrenadier Division's other two regiments north of the gorge, and 212 Volksgrenadier Division in full retreat to the south, 987 Regiment's position had become untenable. They, too, used the cover of darkness to vacate Müllerthal and begin retiring back down the gorge.

This was not the end of the story, though. While 212 Volksgrenadier Division's regiments to the south were pulling back over the Sauer at Bollendorf on Boxing Day, 276 Volksgrenadier Division's new CO, Hugo Dempwolff, still tried hanging on to the west bank. What was desperately important was that the bridge at Dillingen remained intact for at least another day – which it did, despite the efforts of the American artillery and fighter-bombers. Dempwolff later said how relieved he was at the end of the day to find it still standing. His luck did not last, though. A stray shell blasted a hole in it just after nightfall while the last of his troops were trying to cross. Pioniere rushed forward to repair the structure under both artillery and smallarms fire from the American infantry who scented the fox, but the engineers managed to complete the task when the shelling inexplicably eased. The remainder of 987 and the two other regiments made good their escape with a number of vehicles and artillery pieces, after which Dempwolff ordered the bridge to be blown again to delay the enemy.

16/12/1944	17/12	18-19/12	20/12	21/12	22/12	23/12	24/12	25/12	26/12	27/12	28-29/12	30/12	31/12	1/1
pages 28-37,63-66,69-72			38-39		40-42	45-46,80-81	43-44,47-48	82-83		84-85		49-50		

LXXX KORPS' BATTLES

423 Volksgrenadier Regiment

Berdorf/Lauterborn – December 16–20

The grenadiers of I and II Bataillonen, 423 Regiment, of Franz Sensfuss' 212 Volksgrenadier Division, made a successful and relatively uneventful crossing of the Sauer around Bollendorf in the early hours of December 16 and, after quickly overrunning small American outposts along the river line without giving them a chance to radio a warning, advanced rapidly inland. I/423 was on the right, initial destination Berdorf, with II/423 on the left heading for Lauterborn. Behind these villages lay Consdorf and Scheidgen, believed to be American command posts, and behind those again a troublesome artillery position at Altrier. Speed was of the essence but, as so often happened during Seventh Armee's assault, orders to bypass pockets of resistance were partially ignored and both battalions got involved in costly and time-consuming battles for insignificant villages which, at the end of the day, meant they could not achieve their main objectives.

Although Colonel Chance, commander of the U.S. 12th Infantry Regiment, 4th Infantry Division, immediately opposing them, was aware because of reports from the 28th Infantry Division further north that an attack was in progress, the first that he knew of the fact that his own men were threatened was when Company F, II/12th, in Berdorf managed to get a message through at 1015 hrs. By that time the Volksgrenadiers were swarming all over the rugged countryside and had driven one Company F platoon into the shelter of a stone-built farmhouse close to the river. The remainder, about 60-strong, pulled back into the shelter of the strongly built hotel in the middle of the village and prepared to withstand a siege until help arrived. It was a very similar story in Lauterborn, where Company G, also II/12th, soon found itself cut off by the grenadiers of II/423 Volksgrenadier Regiment, who pinned them in a mill on the north side of the village.

Everything in his posture suggesting exhaustion rather than enthusiasm, and not a weapon in sight, a grenadier huddles miserably in the snow.
(U.S. Signal Corps)

On the northern flank of 212 Volksgrenadier Division, so far things were looking good, but the lack of armour support would soon begin to tell.

The CO of 4th Infantry Division, Major-General Raymond Barton, released the 12th Regiment's reserve 1st Battalion to try to stem the rising tide of Volksgrenadiers. Company A with a platoon of light

16/12/1944		17/12	18-19/12	20/12	21/12	22/12	23/12	24/12		25/12	26/12	27/12	28-29/12	30/12	31/12	1/1
pages 28-37,63-66,71-72		67-68		38-39		40-42	45-46,80-81	43-44,47-48	82-83		84-85			49-50		

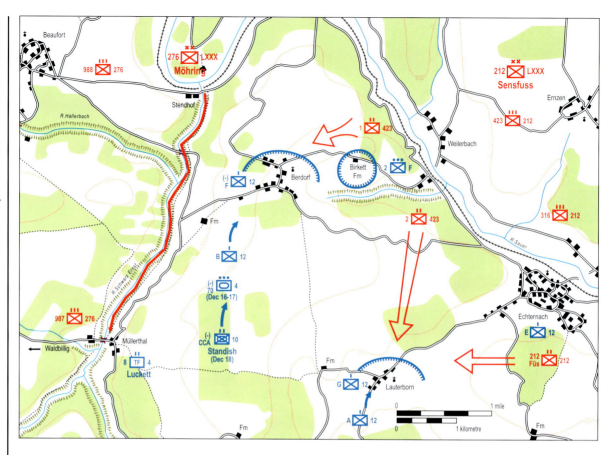

The swift assault by I/ and II/423 Volksgrenadier Regiment completely cut off the small American garrisons in Berdorf and Lauterborn, forcing relief task forces to rescue the survivors.

tanks headed for Lauterborn and Company B with five M4s and five M5s towards Berdorf. In the latter village the grenadiers – who had by now captured all except the hotel – fought them to a standstill and forced them to retire at nightfall. In Lauterborn the GIs had more success and drove the grenadiers out before bivouacking for the night. Next day the Lauterborn force tried to break through to Echternach, where Company E, II/12th, was still holding out, but was unable to succeed. In Berdorf, the relief force reached the hotel but was similarly unable to make any further headway, and meanwhile elements of II/423 Regiment had captured Scheidgen to the southwest. All that stood between them and the American battalion's command post in Consdorf was the regimental anti-tank company. Further help to deny the

grenadiers a victory was, however, on its way.

Combat Command A of Patton's 10th Armored Division was split into three task forces, one of which, as we have seen, tried its luck in the Schwarz Ernst gorge. A second, under Lieutenant-Colonel Miles Standish, reached Berdorf, but I/423's resistance was such that it only managed to recover about 75 yards (69m) of ground. The third, under Lieutenant-Colonel J.R. Riley, recaptured Scheidgen and reached Lauterborn, then got a contingent into Echternach, but the company commander there refused the offer to cover his men's withdrawal, saying he was under orders to stay put. Riley returned to Lauterborn and next day the whole garrison pulled back to Consdorf.

Meanwhile, in Berdorf the battle swayed backwards and forwards with I/423 tenaciously clinging on to a handful of houses at the north end of the village before counter-attacking and recovering most of the lost ground. However, American artillery fire then sent them diving for cover and again the American garrison succeeded in escaping back to Consdorf.

16/12/1944	17/12	18-19/12	20/12	21/12	22/12	23/12	24/12	25/12	26/12	27/12	28-29/12	30/12	31/12	1/1
pages 28-37,63-66,71-72	67-68		38-39		40-42	45-46,80-81	43-44,47-48	82-83		84-85		49-50		

LXXX KORPS' BATTLES
320 Volksgrenadier Regiment and 212 Füsilier Bataillon

Echternach Sector – December 16–19

With his 316 Volksgrenadier Regiment withheld in Armee reserve, the initial assault on LXXX Korps' southern flank was carried solely by Franz Sensfuss' 320 Regiment, 212 Volksgrenadier Division. This gave the regiment a far harder task than that of 423 Regiment on its right, because it had a much broader front to cover defended by elements of both the 2nd and 3rd Battalions of Colonel Chance's 12th Infantry Regiment. Nevertheless, it made deeper inroads into the American lines than its neighbour despite having to choose a different crossing place over the Sauer at the last moment. It was originally intended that the regiment should assault across at the little town of Echternach, which lay in the centre of 212 Volksgrenadier Division's lines, but this plan had to be aborted because the river here was too swollen by rain and snow and too fast flowing for the rubber assault boats. Instead, it had to cross at Edingen to the east with I Bataillon then circling back to Echternach and II/320 striking through Osweiler and Dickweiler towards the American artillery positions between Herborn and Mompach.

Because of the regiment's enforced delay in crossing the Sauer the American companies outposting this stretch of the river were forewarned of the attack and were able to dig in. All that immediately confronted I/320 in Echternach itself was Company E, II/12th Infantry Regiment, but the battalion made no immediate attempt to attack, contenting itself with isolating the defenders and spreading west towards Scheidgen on the flank of II/423. II/320 on the left headed south from Edingen towards Dickweiler, but accurate fire from Company I, III/12th, drove the leading two companies back into the shelter of some woods. When the rest of the battalion caught up, the men reassembled in attack formation for a full-scale assault.

By this time, unfortunately, Colonel Chance had sent his last three M4s to Osweiler, and as the long line of II/320's grenadiers advanced across the open fields, these fell on the battalion's flank while the infantry company in the village poured machine-gun and mortar fire into their ranks. About 50 men, including one company commander, were killed in seconds and the rest broke, running back to the woods. A second company commander and 34 grenadiers surrendered. Deciding any further attempt

Although the precise location cannot be identified, here a typical file of Volksgrenadiers marches towards the front. The landscape is flat, suggesting somewhere quite a way west of the river Sauer.
(U.S. Signal Corps)

16/12/1944		17/12	18-19/12	20/12	21/12	22/12	23/12	24/12		25/12	26/12	27/12	28-29/12	30/12	31/12	1/1
pages 28-37,63-66,69-70		67-68		38-39		40-42	45-46,80-81	43-44,47-48	82-83			84-85		49-50		

71

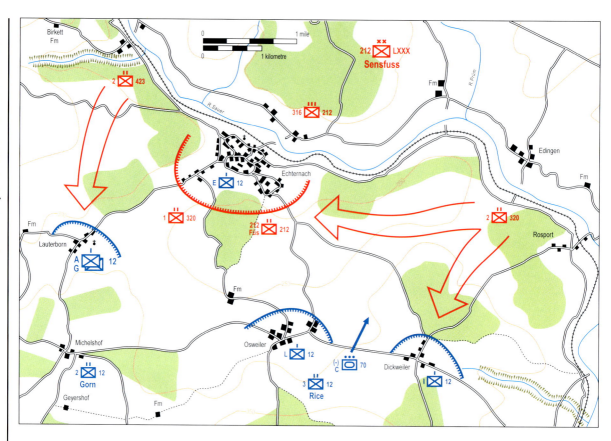

The attack by 320 Volksgrenadier Regiment was delayed by the necessity to move the bridging site from Echternach to Edingen and although Echternach was finally taken on December 19, all efforts to capture Dickweiler and Osweiler failed.

at a frontal assault was fruitless, the battalion commander rallied his men and that night sent them out to the flanks to surround both villages. The company commander in Dickweiler radioed 'Situation desperate' so Colonel Chance committed his last remaining reserve, Company C, I/12th, to their aid. They had a running battle with elements of II/320 and one platoon was wiped out, but the remainder made it into the village.

Meanwhile, further American reinforcements were arriving almost hourly, including the 2nd Battalion of 4th Infantry Division's 22nd Regiment. Company F fought its way through II/320 to reinforce Dickweiler still further but Companies E and G ran into a strong contingent of I/320 south of Osweiler. In the mêlée they got separated and dug in for the night. With more M4s of both the 19th and 70th Tank Battalions now

moving in to Osweiler and Dickweiler, however, the villages had become impregnable to a single battalion assault, and 212 Volksgrenadier Division's CO, General Sensfuss, ordered II/320 onto the defensive.

While these encounters on the division's left had been going on, I/320 had tightened its noose around Echternach. An attempt to put bridging spans over the old stone piers was foiled by American artillery fire, as was a later attempt to build a pontoon bridge, but on December 19 the pioniere finally managed to complete one suitable for armour and artillery at Edingen. One of the division's handful of StuGs was sent to reinforce the grenadiers of I/320 besieging Echternach, along with the division's Füsilier Bataillon, and that night Sensfuss personally led an assault against the hat factory where Company E, II/12th, had holed up. While the StuG poured fire into the building, the grenadiers and füsiliers attacked from all sides, using satchel charges and Panzerfausts to blast holes in the walls. After a short but intense fight the American company commander surrendered, along with his remaining 132 men.

16/12/1944	17/12	18-19/12	20/12	21/12	22/12	23/12	24/12	25/12	26/12	27/12	28-29/12	30/12	31/12	1/1
pages 28-37,63-66,69-70	67-68		38-39		40-42	45-46,80-81	43-44,47-48	82-83		84-85		49-50		

SEVENTH ARMEE

LIII KORPS

From commanding the smallest and least significant Korps in the whole of Heeresgruppe B at the beginning of operation 'Herbstnebel', General der Kavallerie Friedrich-Wilhelm von Rothkirch was thrust into the position of having to try to control the most powerful Korps in the whole of Seventh Armee – after everything had gone wrong, of course! It is every commander's nightmare, to be asked to restore order in a situation not of his own devising, on unfamiliar ground and with officers and troops who are strangers with unknown capabilities. Under the circumstances it is thus to von Rothkirch's credit that he coped as well as he did.

LIII Korps itself had first been formed late in 1940 and fought on the central sector of the Russian front from 1941 to July 1944, when it was virtually destroyed at Vitebsk. The Generalkommando 'von Rothkirch', which had been conducting security and anti-partisan operations in the Korps rear, was pulled back to Danzig and on November 11 took over a reconstituted LIII Korps on the western front. On December 16, however, it was a Korps in name only and the troops under command comprised merely a penal battalion of infantry and a static machine-gun battalion. These had no active role in operation 'Herbstnebel' and were assigned purely defensive and insignificant positions on Seventh Armee's southern flank west of LIII Korps' HQ in Trier, along the steep river banks at the confluence of the Sauer/Saar and Moselle/Mosel. Six days into the new offensive, however, General von Rothkirch and his staff were given a new and much more demanding task.

By December 21, Generalmajor Ludwig Heilmann's 5 Fallschirm Division (LXXXV Korps) had accomplished its objectives and was blocking the anticipated routes up which Patton's tanks would roll to the relief of Bastogne. However, the paras were thinly spread and widely separated from the men of Generalmajor Erich Schmidt's 352 Volksgrenadier Division who were still struggling to advance on their southeastern flank. On December 22, therefore – by coincidence, the

---

LIII KORPS
General der Kavallerie Freidrich-Wilhelm von Rothkirch
Stab

---

5 Fallshirm Division (Heilmann)
  (from LXXXV Korps December 22)
9 Volksgrenadier Division (Kolb)
  (from OKW Reserve December 22)
Führer Grenadier Brigade (Kahler)
  (from OKW Reserve December 22)
15 Panzergrenadier Division (Deckert)
  (from XLVII Korps, Fifth Panzer Armee, January 18-20)
79 Volksgrenadier Division
  (from LXXXV Korps, January 18-20)
276 Volksgrenadier Division (Möhring/Dempwolff)
  (from LXXX Korps, January 18-20)
44 Festungs-Maschinengewhr Bataillon
  (from Armee Reserve December 22)
XIII/999 Festungs-Infanterie Bataillon
  (from Armee Reserve December 22)

General von Rothkirch looks suitably bemused after his capture by men of the U.S. 4th Armored Division in March 1945. The expression is very understandable given the situation he had to confront south of Bastogne.
(U.S. Army)

same day that Ob West issued the orders for operation 'Nordwind' in Alsace – Model took the bold step of moving von Rothkirch and his staff from the left to the right of Seventh Armee's flanks and entrusting him with command of the Fallschirmjäger, plus Oberst Werner Kolb's 9 Volksgrenadier Division and Oberst Hans-Joachim Kahler's Führer Grenadier Brigade,

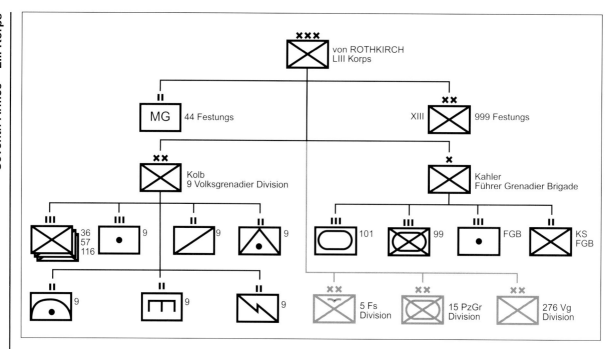

which were released from OKW reserve at the same time. This rearrangement shortened LXXXV Korps' overstretched lines but left General Baptist Kniess with only one division, 352 Volksgrenadier, until the arrival of Oberst Alois Weber's 79 Volksgrenadier Division, which was released from Heeresgruppe B reserve on the same date.

Being almost fully motorised, the Führer Grenadier Brigade was first to begin arriving. However, it was strung out over miles of road stretching far to the east. For von Rothkirch, in his new headquarters in Wiltz, it was another nightmare. The brigade constituted the only real armoured strength in the whole of Seventh Armee apart from 11 Sturmgeschutz Brigade (attached to 5 Fallschirm Division), and could almost certainly have been utilised more fruitfully if Brandenberger had allowed von Rothkirch time to assemble it for a determined counter-attack.

However, it was the perilous situation of Heilmann's lightly equipped 5 Fallschirm Division to the south of Bastogne which concerned Brandenberger, so Kahler's brigade was thrown into the battle in bits and pieces as it arrived, and suffered as horribly as you might expect, despite the assistance of Weber's 79 Volksgrenadier Division on its left flank. (This division did not have so far to travel as 9 Volksgrenadier Division and was in place on LXXXV Korps' right flank 24 hours after receiving its mobilisation order. Later, it was also added to von Rothkirch's command, but not until after the middle of January 1945, by which time it was far too late to salvage much at all.)

Plodding along on foot in the wake of 'FGB', Kolb's 9 Volksgrenadier Division did not arrive until days later, when von Rothkirch was at least able to deploy it to relieve the Führer Grenadier Brigade and try to re-assemble a mobile reserve. In the meanwhile, however, both 5 Fallschirm Division and the Führer Grenadier Brigade had been heavily engaged.

By another coincidence, Patton began the U.S. Third Army's counter-offensive on the same day that von Rothkirch assumed command of Seventh Armee's right flank, December 22. Patton's immediate objectives were to relieve the beleaguered 101st Airborne in Bastogne and drive the German forces now commanded by von Rothkirch back across the river Sûre. The attack was spearheaded by Major-General John Millikin's III Corps, with 4th Armored

When von Rothkirch assembled his staff at Wiltz on December 22, 5 Fallschirm Division was thinly spread in a long line from the Neufchâteau–Bastogne road in the west to Liefrange in the east and seriously delayed 4th Armored Division's advance. The Führer Grenadier Brigade moved into the vacuum on its left but was itself over-extended on the line Arsdorf–Bourscheid. By the time 9 Volksgrenadier Division arrived at the end of the month, Bastogne had already been relieved and Patton's men were across the Sûre and pressing towards Wiltz. The map also shows Generalleutnant Karl Decker's XXXIX Panzer Korps' attack at Lutrebois and Villers-la-Bonne-Eau on December 30 in which 14 Fallschirm Regiment took part.

Division heading more or less in a straight line north from Arlon. The 26th Infantry Division was in the Corps' centre, with the 80th on its right anchored on the river Alzette. The American attack thus hit elements of both LIII and LXXXV Korps as well as 26 Volksgrenadier Division from XLVII Panzer Korps of Fifth Army which was the principal formation involved in the siege of Bastogne.

Falling back slowly from Martelange and Burnon to Warnach and Chaumont, 5 Fallschirm Division and its attached StuGs so delayed CCA and CCB of 4th Armored Division that Patton switched CCR – which had also been stalled by the paras at Bigonville – to III Corps' left, and on December 26 its leading elements broke through 26 Volksgrenadier Division's cordon at Assenois to reach Bastogne.

Thrown hastily into battle on December 23, the Führer Grenadier Brigade's leading elements had reached as far west as Eschdorf and Arsdorf where they met the 26th Infantry Division's 328th Regiment. The grenadiers' determined resistance in these two villages held the Americans up until December 26, but they were forced to abandon Heiderscheid and failed to retake it in a combined attack with 79 Volksgrenadier Division on the 24th. Falling back to the partially demol- ished bridge over the Sûre at Heiderscheidergrund, the brigade defended the crossing in force but the U.S.

101st Infantry Regiment outflanked them and threw a Bailey bridge across the river at Bonnal. The grenadiers then counter-attacked unsuccessfully at Kaundorf before being taken into reserve following the belated arrival of 9 Volksgrenadier Division, which was committed to action on December 30.

Part of 5 Fallschirm Division was involved in XXXIX Panzer Korps' counter-attack to try to break the Bastogne corridor at Lutrebois and Villers-la-Bonne-Eau on the same day, but this was the last throw, and the remainder of LIII Korps' war was not a happy one. Although later reinforced by both 79 and the remnants of 276 Volksgrenadier Divisions, von Rothkirch had to abandon Wiltz and fall back behind the river Our during January.

After that it was a by now familiar story. When Patton's Third and Courtney Hodges' First U.S. Armies launched their major counter-offensive on January 3, all hope of capturing Bastogne evaporated and the 'bulge' rapidly shrank to a 'pimple' west of Vianden. LIII Korps continued to fight hard as it fell back towards the Rhein during February. However, after von Rothkirch walked into captivity at the beginning of March 1945 – mistaking tanks of the 4th Armored Division for German because there were clusters of prisoners around them – the remnants of his force were destroyed in the Ruhr pocket just a month later.

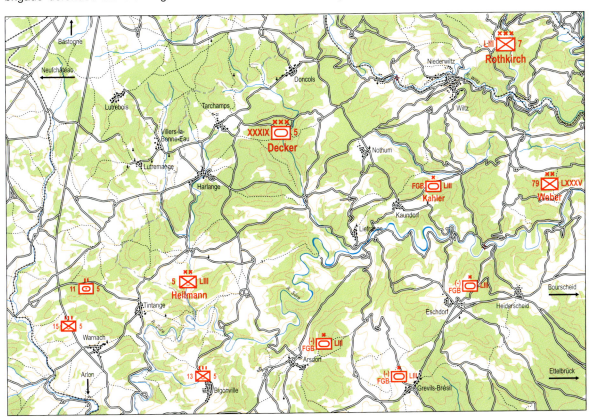

9 Volksgrenadier Division

L ike 167 Volksgrenadier Division, Oberst Werner Kolb's 9th was not released from OKW reserve until December 22 and, when it arrived on the battlefield, was far 'too little and too late' to affect events in any material way. Originally designated like the 167th for Fifth Panzer Armee, Model instead handed it over to Brandenberger's Seventh because of the critical situation south of Bastogne. However, by the time 9 Volksgrenadier Division arrived in the vicinity of Wiltz from its assembly area at Gerolstein a week later – having been forced to move up by night marches because of Allied air attacks – the U.S. 26th Infantry Division was already across the Sûre and steadily forcing the Führer Grenadier Brigade back after its abortive counter-attack at Kaundorf.

The division first went into action just north of Nothum on December 30 and, using every tree and contour of the ground as cover, as well as launching several localised counter-attacks, seriously delayed the approach of the Americans towards Wiltz, although an entire company of 140 men was forced to surrender southwest of the little town during the afternoon. Kolb's men counter-attacked again in the evening and inflicted heavy casualties on both the 101st and 104th U.S. Infantry Regiments. The next two days were relatively quiet, but on January 2 the division fought the American reserve 328th Regiment to a standstill, giving a brief reprieve to 5 Fallschirm

Division to its northwest in what had become known as the 'Harlange pocket'. In the end, however, as down all the German line, courage and determination were no answer to the U.S. superiority in manpower and matériel, particularly in artillery, and by the middle of the month the division was back behind the Our.

The original 9 Infanterie Division was formed when conscription was re-introduced by Hitler in 1935 and

Pandemonium in a farmyard at Nothum when a shell which might well have come from one of 9 Volksgrenadier Division's Volks-Artillerie Regiment's guns destroys a Jeep belonging to the U.S. 104th Infantry Regiment, 26th Infantry Division. A few of the farmer's horses were killed in the same explosion.
(U.S. Signal Corps)

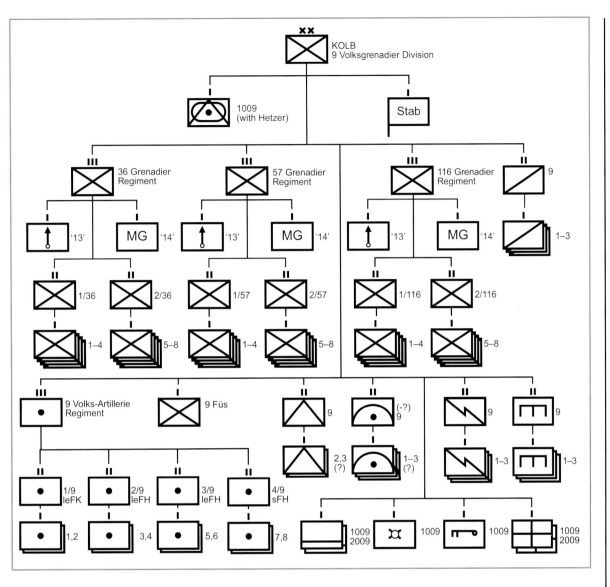

principally comprised men from Hesse and Nassau, with its home station in Wehrkreis IX at Giessen. In 1939 it was on the Saar front alongside 212 Infanterie Division, but for the campaign in the west it was transferred to Panzergruppe 'von Kleist' on the left flank of von Rundstedt's Heeresgruppe A.

Commanded by Generalleutnant Graf Siegmund von Schleinitz, the division was next assigned to Heeresgruppe Süd for the invasion of Russia and spent the next three years on this front, taking part in the drive through the Ukraine and the momentous battle of Kiev in the summer of 1941. The following year it took part in the long advance to the Caucasus and, avoiding entrapment at Stalingrad, was withdrawn into the Kuban bridgehead alongside 79 Infanterie Division in 1943. Withdrawn by sea to the Crimea, the 9th was at less than half strength by October but was kept in the line on the lower Dniepr. Slowly forced back during the Soviet winter counter-offensive, the 9th – now commanded by Generalmajor Werner Gebb – suffered the same fate as the 79th when Romania capitulated and was practically destroyed alongside most of Mieth's unfortunate IV Korps.

The new 9 Volksgrenadier Division commanded by Oberst Werner Kolb was activated on October 13 at Esjberg on the west coast of Denmark by simply renumbering the partially formed 584 Volksgrenadier Division. The 9th was still understrength when it detrained at Gerolstein on December 19, despite which it fought gamely against Patton's men but by the end of March 1945 consisted of little more than Kolb and his staff. The remnants were absorbed by 352 Volksgrenadier Division in April and surrendered outside Nürnberg.

Führer Grenadier Brigade

Both the Führer Grenadier Brigade and its older sibling, the Führer Begleit Brigade, were held in OKW Reserve at the beginning of the new offensive, and both might have fared considerably better if they had been released to Heeresgruppe B earlier and committed to battle at full strength instead of arriving piecemeal.

The original Führer Grenadier Bataillon had been

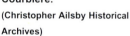

Oberst Hans-Joachim Kahler had no chance to prove his talent as a field commander because he was wounded by a shell splinter on December 23 and his place taken by his deputy, Major von Courbière.
(Christopher Ailsby Historical Archives)

FÜHRER GRENADIER BRIGADE

Oberst Hans-Joachim Kahler/
Major von Courbière

Stabs Kompanie

---

101 Panzer Regiment
99 Panzergrenadier Regiment
Artillerie Regiment 'FGB' (-)
911 Sturmgeschutz Brigade
124 Flak Abteilung
Kampfschule 'FGB'
1124 Infantriegeschutz Kompanie
1124 Panzerjäger Kompanie
1124 Panzer Aufklärungs Kompanie
1124 Flak Kompanie
1124 Pionier Kompanie
1124 Nachrichten Abteilung
Nachschub Truppe 'FGB'
Werkstatt Kompanie 'FGB'
Sanitäts Kompanie 'FGB'

---

raised in East Prussia in April 1943 as a second guard unit for the outer perimeter of the *Wolfsschanze* at Rastenburg, but the bulk of its men were soon committed to battle on the Russian front as part of the 'Großdeutschland' Division. A year later the battalion was reorganised at Fallsingbostel as an armoured brigade, drawing its personnel from the hand-picked 'GD' pool, and in October was assigned to XXVII Korps of Fourth Armee to help contain a Soviet attack south of Gumbinnen. Operating in conjunction with both 5 Panzer and the 'Hermann Göring' Divisions, the brigade repelled the Russians at Daken and Großwaltersdorf over October 21-23 but suffered heavy casualties and a month later was withdrawn to Cottbus to refit.

When it was sent west under the temporary command of Oberst Hans-Joachim Kahler between December 11 and 17 the brigade's composition did not match any standard configuration, but in armour it was stronger than some Panzer divisions. The 101st Panzer Regiment 'FGB' comprised a single battalion of five companies, the first three with 12 Panthers each, the fourth with 11 Jagdpanzer IV/70s and the fifth with 14 StuG IIIs. In place of a second battalion,

the regiment had 911 Sturmgeschutz Brigade attached with three companies totalling 31 StuGs. The brigade thus had a total of 92 AFVs!

The 99th Panzergrenadier Regiment comprised three battalions. The Panzer Füsilier Bataillon had three rifle companies and a support company, all mounted in SdKfz 251 half-tracks. The Grenadier Bataillon was unarmoured but fully motorised, with three rifle companies, a machine-gun and a towed infantry gun company, while 929 Infanterie Bataillon zbv had three bicycle-equipped rifle companies and a motorised support company. Further support was provided by the armoured cars of the Aufklärungs Kompanie and the 15cm sIG 33s of the Infanteriegeschutz Kompanie. However, the brigade's Artillerie Regiment 'FGB' was understrength, some of its guns having been loaned to Otto Skorzeny's 150 Panzer Brigade. Total manpower was around 6,000, but many of the replacements received in November were only partially trained.

Nevertheless, it was a very powerful fighting force and its appearance in the Ardennes alongside the Führer Begleit Brigade further north at St Vith caused the Allies a great deal of anxiety, not least because they feared they faced the whole of the elite 'Großdeutschland' Division despite the fact that the Russians told them otherwise!

Unfortunately, the brigade's performance did not fully match up to expectations – which was not the fault of its men but of the way they were committed to the battle in dribs and drabs as the various elements arrived, so Kahler was unable to utilise their full pot-ential. When Model released the brigade to Brandenberger on December 22, it was sent to bolster Seventh Armee's right flank in the face of Patton's III Corps' counter-attack from the south. The brigade had to struggle through the usual traffic snarl trying to cross the Sûre at Pont, and on the 23rd was strung out in 'penny packets' on the line Bourscheid–Heiderscheid–Eschdorf–Arsdorf. It thus met the advance of the U.S. 26th and 80th Infantry Divisions in fragments, and although it held on tenaciously at Eschdorf, it was forced to give up Heiderscheid and fall back on Heiderscheidergrund, where the bridge over the Sûre had been partially demolished. Oberst Kahler was badly wounded by a shell splinter that evening and

his deputy, Major von Courbière, took over until the belated arrival of Generalmajor Hellmuth Mader.

Next day, elements of the Panzer Füsilier Bataillon counter-attacked from Eschdorf towards Heider-scheid, in conjunction with a dawn attack by the newly arrived 79 Volksgrenadier Division (see LXXXV Korps), but as on so many occasions during the whole Ardennes offensive, American artillery fire proved the decisive factor in the battle. As the 26th Infantry Division kept up the pressure, the bulk of the brigade retired behind the Sûre, its place in the line being taken over by 9 Volksgrenadier Division. The brigade counter-attacked unsuccessfully at Kaundorf on December 27, then retired slowly through Wiltz.

Pulled out of the western front early in January 1945, the brigade was enlarged on paper to constitute the Führer Grenadier Division – still commanded by Hellmuth Mader – and assigned to Heeresgruppe Vistula. In April it was re-allocated to 'Sepp' Dietrich's Sixth SS-Panzer Armee and finally surrendered to American troops outside Vienna in May.

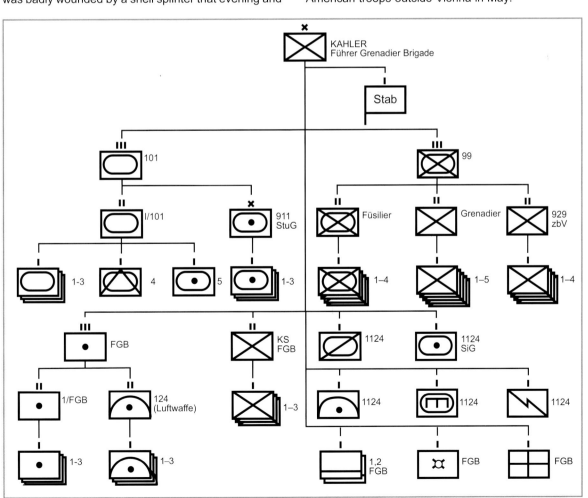

LIII KORPS' BATTLES
Führer Grenadier Brigade

Arsdorf/Eschdorf/Grevils-Brésil – December 23–25

The biggest problem faced by Oberst Hans-Joachim Kahler's Führer Grenadier Brigade, as noted previously, is that it was committed to battle piecemeal and unable to launch a full-scale counter-attack against either of the American III Corps' divisions it ran up against, the 26th in the west and the 80th in the east. Called out of OKW Reserve on December 22, the brigade was originally intended to cross the Sûre at Ettelbruck and then head directly to the support of 5 Fallschirm Division around Martelange, but the threat posed to Ettelbruck by the arrival of the U.S. 80th Infantry Division caused this to be amended. Instead, the brigade would try to fill the vacuum between the Fallschirmjäger and 352 Volksgrenadier Division.

Leading elements of the brigade crossed the Our at Roth, delayed by the fact that the bridge had been damaged by Allied aerial attacks and the roads were blocked by miles of traffic jams, then the Sûre below Lipperscheid, and advanced through Bourscheid to begin assembling around Eschdorf and Heiderscheid. By December 23 all that had arrived was 1124 Aufklärungs Kompanie, the armoured Füsilier Bataillon of 99 Panzergrenadier Regiment, the first two companies of 101 Panzer Regiment's Panthers and a company of StuGs from 911 Sturmgeschutz Brigade. Kahler put one company of füsiliers apiece into Eschdorf and Heiderscheid and sent two south with a platoon of Panthers to Grevils-Brésil, hoping to establish contact with the leading 915 Regiment of 352 Volksgrenadier Division. A squad was also sent to Arsdorf on the brigade's western flank.

The tiny garrison in Arsdorf was quickly evicted with the arrival from the south at dusk of the 1st Battalion, 328th Regiment, 26th Infantry Division. This then swung east to the assistance of the 3rd Battalion, which had been stopped in its tracks by the much stronger force in Grevils-Brésil.

The American divisional commander, Major-General Willard Paul, had decided earlier that the ground was unsuitable for tanks so for once it was the GIs who had no armoured support. Nor did a half-hour artillery barrage during the night shift Kahler's men, but at daybreak the arrival of the 390th AAA Battalion with armoured half-tracks mounting quick-firing 37mm cannon and quadruple .50 cal machine-guns finally drove the German garrison out. Their direct line of retreat had been blocked because the 328th's commander, Colonel Ben Jacobs, had leapfrogged Grevils-Brésil by sending his 2nd Battalion looping round towards Eschdorf. The füsiliers therefore split up into small parties and headed cross-country towards Dellen.

The FGB company in Heiderscheid also had its hands full during the night of December 23. After the 1st Battalion of the American 319th Regiment had so fortuitously sliced through 915 Volksgrenadier Regiment on the Merzig road, it headed on through Oberfeulen towards Kehmen. The following 2nd Battalion debussed in Oberfeulen and advanced on foot towards Heiderscheid. Here, Kahler's men were wide awake and, as the line of GIs approached the village across the snow-covered fields, they were silhouetted by the bright moonlight. Waiting until they were sure of their targets, the füsiliers, and a supporting StuG, opened fire, forcing the American battalion's leading two companies to dive for cover.

Two factors altered the situation. A pair of M4s moved up in support of the attack, but were checked by a minefield south of the village. Then a lucky artillery shell blew a path through it and, engaging the StuG at close range, they blew it apart. The American infantry now surged into the village and, although a hand-to-hand struggle lasted most of the morning, by midday the last of the füsiliers had pulled back to

16/12/1944		17/12	18-19/12	20/12	21/12	22/12	23/12	24/12	25/12	26/12	27/12	28-29/12	30/12	31/12	1/1
pages 28-37,63-66,69-72		67-68		38-39		40-42	45-46	43-44,47-48	82-83		84-85		49-50		

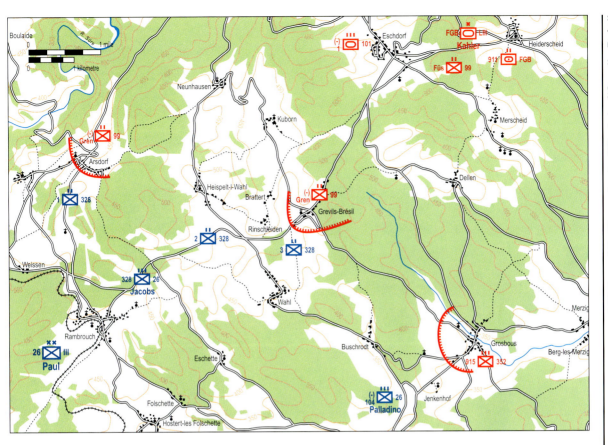

The Führer Grenadier Brigade was unable to deploy effectively in the Eschdorf area and, because it lacked its artillery and grenadier battalions, was unable to resist the powerful III Corps' onslaught to the south of the Sûre.

Eschdorf. Here, they were rallied by the acting brigade commander, Major von Courbière, for a counter-attack. Kahler himself had been badly wounded earl-ier in the night during a reconnaissance, and the lack of experienced leadership over the next few days would have an adverse effect on the brigade's performance.

Courbière managed to assemble the best part of two infantry companies for the attack, followed by a company of 11 Panthers. Momentarily, success seemed in sight because a number of Americans could be seen fleeing. However, the remainder stayed firm and two Panthers succumbed to bazooka rounds. Then a platoon of M36 tank destroyers arrived and knocked out four more, while a seventh was disabled by one of the M4s. The surviving tanks withdrew,

followed by the infantry.

At Eschdorf, meanwhile, the 2nd Battalion of the 328th Regiment which had hooked round Grevils-Brésil arrived a mile or so south of Eschdorf. In the village, Major von Courbière had eagerly welcomed the arrival of three battalions of Alois Weber's 79 Volksgrenadier Division, two of which were being hastily organised for another counter-attack at Heiderscheid on the morning of Christmas Eve. The American battalion therefore ran into a much fiercer fusilade of fire than had been expected as it approached Eschdorf, and went to ground. Their commander wanted to withdraw, but was refused permission because the III Corps commander, General Millikin, badly wanted Eschdorf.

The 1st Battalion of the 26th Infantry Division's 104th Regiment therefore began marching to II/328th's aid. During the night, however, Companies E, F and G, with three M4s for support, attacked the village from three sides. The German garrison, now seriously understrength, fought gamely but at nightfall Courbière and Weber pulled them out.

16/12/1944		17/12	18-19/12	20/12	21/12	22/12	23/12	24/12	25/12	26/12	27/12	28-29/12	30/12	31/12	1/1
pages 28-37,63-66,69-72		67-68		38-39		40-42	45-46	43-44,47-48	82-83		84-85		49-50		

LIII KORPS' BATTLES
Führer Grenadier Brigade

Heiderscheidergrund – December 25–27

Thoroughly disappointed at his own men's inability to recapture Heiderscheid on December 23, and that of Alois Weber's two battalions from 79 Volksgrenadier Division on Christmas Eve, coupled with the failure in regaining contact with the two companies driven out of Grevils-Brésil, Major von Courbière could see no alternative but to withdraw the Führer Grenadier Brigade to a more easily defensible position north of the river Sûre. This, after all, is where the brigade was originally supposed to have been deployed. On top of everything else, the brigade's missing Panzer and Jagdpanzer companies had run into American tanks and tank destroyers outside Kehmen while moving west from Bourscheid and been forced to retrace their tracks.

If von Courbière could reunite his depleted forces with those, and the Grenadier Bataillon immediately behind them, perhaps he could retrieve something from the situation after all. However, General Brandenberger wanted the defence to continue south of the river and only agreed to its displacement north after the loss of Eschdorf, with the result that the brigade did not begin redeploying effectively until the early hours of December 26.

The Americans had a limited choice of crossing points over the Sûre along this stretch, so von Courbière put an outpost in Liefrange overlooking Bonnal on his right flank and mustered the bulk of the brigade behind Esch-sur-Sûre and Heiderscheider-grund. (From this point on, unfortunately, it is virtually impossible to decipher which components of the brigade were exactly where.) His left flank, von Courbière must have felt, was relatively secure with Weber's Volksgrenadiers now well entrenched around Bourscheid, although they still needed to take the high ground at Ringelerhof – a goal which was to ultimately elude them even after the loan of FGB's

artillery battalion when it eventually caught up.

The main immediate threat appeared to be the 319th Regiment of the 80th Infantry Division which was now securely in place between Heiderscheid and Tadler. On this regiment's left, however, the 26th Infantry Division was also driving hard towards the river while American artillery plastered the terrain north of Eschdorf where small rearguards of FGB sought to buy time for the brigade to regroup. The bridge at Heiderscheidergrund, which a couple of American companies had had under observation for three days, became von Courbière's priority, and the bulk of the brigade was assembled behind it while pioniere blew the crossing. This caused the Americans to look for alternatives at Bonnal and Esch-sur-Sûre.

At Bonnal the FGB defenders met the leading companies of III/101st Regiment, 26th Infantry Division, with such a fusilade that they sought a crossing further west. When I/101st then appeared, however, the German pickets withdrew, so the Americans now had two crossing points to the west of Esch-sur-Sûre and Heiderscheidergrund. Major von Courbière's eyes were, however, firmly fixed on the latter, because if the GIs got across here they had immediate access to the main road towards Wiltz and LIII Korps' field headquarters.

Under pressure to re-establish a foothold south of the Sûre, FGB pioniere threw a trestle over the span of the bridge they had earlier demolished. A first attempt by some of the brigade's tanks to get across was stopped short by shellfire, but on the second try four Panthers and a StuG managed to gain a toehold. It was very shortlived because a barrage of white phosphorus shells forced the crews to abandon their vehicles hastily.

Meanwhile, the U.S. 101st Regiment had been expanding its Bonnal bridgehead and captured

16/12/1944		17/12	18-19/12	20/12	21/12	22/12	23/12	24/12		25/12	26/12	27/12	28-29/12	30/12	31/12	1/1
pages 28-37,63-66,69-72		67-68		38-39		40-42	45-46,80-81	43-44,47-48				84-85		49-50		

Liefrange. Major von Courbière retaliated by sending what remained of his Füsilier Bataillon and the Grenadier Bataillon with a few tanks into a counter-attack at 0720 hrs on December 27. Although the GIs were outnumbered, and the two German battalions momentarily ruled the battlefield, they called down artillery fire from all the 26th Division's batteries and, as so often, the assault disintegrated in bloody chaos. Later in the morning, the 1st Battalion of the 104th joined the 101st across the Bonnal bridge then swung east towards Esch-sur-Sûre, while the 2nd Battalion, well supported by the divisional artillery,

The battle along the banks of the river Sûre around Heiderscheidergrund was confused, with elements of two American divisions involved, Major von Courbière trying to regroup the Führer Grenadier Brigade in a defensible position which was soon outflanked, and the supporting battalions of 79 Volksgrenadier Division moving through their lines to new positions around Bourscheid for the ill-fated assault on Ringelerhof.

put on a demonstration at Heiderscheidergrund to convince von Courbière that a major assault was about to take place there. The ploy worked and while the Führer Grenadier Brigade remained pinned in place, American engineers constructed a second bridge at Esch and tank destroyers began trundling over to reinforce the three infantry battalions now firmly established north of the river.

Although the American bridgehead was secure and threatening his right flank, Major von Courbière's position was not as desperate as it might have seemed because the U.S. 26th Infantry Division was now fighting entirely on its own. The 35th, which was moving into position on its left, was not yet in place and had been forced to deploy in line facing the Lutrebois–Villers-la-Bonne-Eau–Harlange sector, while the 80th on its right was deeply enmeshed in its own battle against 79 Volksgrenadier Division. Nevertheless, von Courbière must have welcomed the arrival of Generalmajor Helmuth Mader to take over command for the next phase.

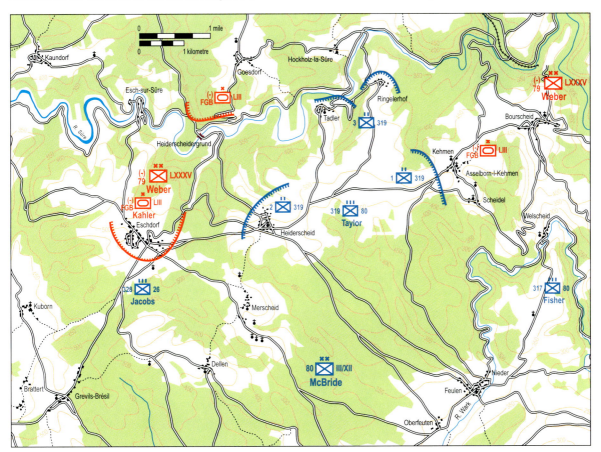

16/12/1944		17/12	18-19/12	20/12	21/12	22/12	23/12	24/12		25/12	26/12	27/12	28-29/12	30/12	31/12	1/1
pages 28-37,63-66,69-72		67-68		38-39		40-42	45-46,80-81	43-44,47-48				84-85		49-50		

LIII KORPS' BATTLES
Führer Grenadier Brigade and 9 Volksgrenadier Division

Kaundorf/Wiltz – December 27–30

While Generalmajor Helmuth Mader was familiarising himself with his officers and the Führer Grenadier Brigade's exposed position north of Heiderscheidergrund bridge, he could see from their maps that the American 26th Infantry Division was restricted in its choice of expanding its bridgehead to three very narrow and poorly surfaced roads dominated by the villages of Liefrange, Bavigne and Kaundorf. Since the recapture of Wiltz was the enemy's obvious intention, and they had already hung tenaciously on at Liefrange, this made Kaundof, and the village of Nothum slightly to its north, the key positions to defend. Once again, fortunately – as in the 'Bourscheid Triangle' defended by 79 Volksgrenadier Division – the terrain lay in the defenders' favour. On top of this Mader also knew that further help was on its way with the release of Oberst Werner Kolb's

9 Volksgrenadier Division from OKW Reserve, even though this was not expected to begin arriving at Wiltz from its assembly area at Gerolstein for at least a couple of days because of Allied air interdiction attacks.

Von Courbière had already repelled one attack at Kaundorf, where two companies of the U.S. 3rd Battalion, 101st Regiment, accompanied by a platoon of Shermans, had tried to seize the high ground. Half the American tanks had been knocked out and the remainder of the assault force beat a hasty retreat. Not for long, however. During the night of December 27/28, I/101st attacked at Bavigne, but Mader's men held firm until late in the morning. In the intervening time, III/101st had returned to the attack and finally fought their way through Kaundorf, while the 2nd Battalion leapfrogged to within sight of Nothum. The sight of Führer Grenadier Brigade tanks here halted

Although the Americans enjoyed most of the 'spoils of war', the men of the Volksgrenadier divisions availed themselves of every opportunity to press abandoned enemy vehicles into their own service. Here a grenadier examines an apparently intact M3 armoured half-track ambulance to see whether it will still run.

(U.S. Signal Corps)

16/12/1944		17/12	18-19/12	20/12	21/12	22/12	23/12	24/12		25/12	26/12	27/12	28-29/12	30/12	31/12	1/1
pages 28-37,63-66,69-72		67-68		38-39		40-42	45-46,80-81	43-44,47-48		82-83				49-50		

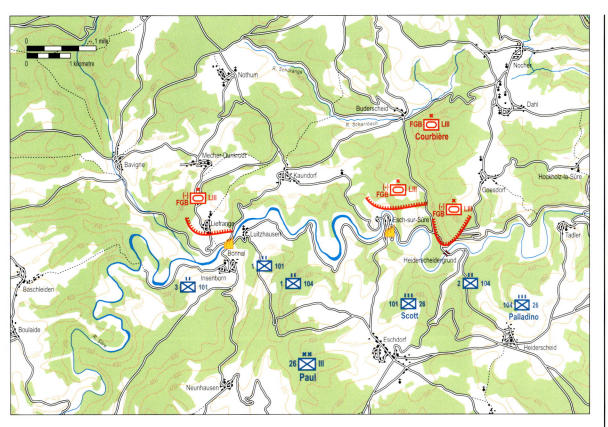

Although the town of Wiltz was only four miles (6.5km) away as the crow flies once the U.S. 26th Infantry Division established itself on the north bank of the Sûre, the combined efforts of the Führer Grenadier Brigade and the freshly arrived 9 Volksgrenadier Division made those miles very long indeed.

their progress for several hours on December 28, but at the end of the day the arrival of M4s and tank destroyers forced the defenders to pull back towards Wiltz.

The Führer Grenadier Brigade was necessarily responding to the American initiative at this point, and the capture of Kaundorf threatening the flank forced General Mader to decamp from Buderscheid when it came under assault by the 2nd Battalion of the 104th Infantry Regiment. Then came a welcome reprieve. American intelligence had somehow got wind of a supposed major counter-attack and ordered the CO of 26th Infantry Division, Major-General Willard Paul, to go over to the defensive on the 29th. When, by mid-morning, the counter-attack had failed to materialise, Paul ordered his two regiments to press

on. Massed artillery had already been firing all night at Wiltz, where LIII Korps' commander, Friedrich-Wilhelm von Roth-kirch, had established his headquarters, and now the American infantry began pushing across the heavily forested ridges.

The Führer Grenadier Brigade's infantry strength by this time was badly depleted, and for the most part Mader made use of his remaining Panzers, plus Nebelwerfers from Armee reserve, to slow their advance. Both the U.S. 101st and 104th Regiments found themselves constantly pinned down and unable to advance more than yards at a time. Moreover, the leading elements of Kolb's 9 Volksgrenadier Division had begun arriving, although their first encounter with the Americans on December 30 was hardly encouraging because a whole company was isolated and forced to surrender. However, the remainder of the battalion (which is uncertain) counter-attacked with the help of a few FGB Panzers and stalled the 101st Regiment in its tracks, while the remnants of Mader's brigade similarly halted the 104th north of Buderscheid. At this point the brigade was, however, pulled back to Wiltz to regroup, leaving the battlefield to the Volksgrenadiers.

16/12/1944	17/12	18-19/12	20/12	21/12	22/12	23/12	24/12	25/12	26/12	27/12	28-29/12	30/12	31/12	1/1
pages 28-37,63-66,69-72	67-68		38-39		40-42	45-46,80-81	43-44,47-48	82-83				49-50		

FIRST ARMEE

OPERATION 'NORDWIND'

Quite why Hitler decided upon a second new offensive in the west when it was already becoming apparent that 'Herbstnebel' was not going according to plan is not clear – but many of his decisions, particularly since the bomb plot in July, were irrational. Partly, at least, it was psychological: the recapture of Alsace, and in particular of the city of Strasbourg, would be a morale booster to the German people, who were weary of the war and, especially, of the long string of defeats since the end of 1942. Partly it was opportunistic, because OKW had predicted that much of the strength of Patton's Third Army would have to be stripped from the line to help contain the situation in the Ardennes, thus leaving the Saarbrücken sector significantly weakened.

Partly, too, Hitler must have hoped that a southpaw body punch would take some of the heat off Heeresgruppe B in the Ardennes, and at the same time delay any movement of American troops north to the Ninth Army sector for the attack the Allies were obviously planning towards the Ruhr. What is most strange about 'Nordwind', and the Luftwaffe's operation 'Bodenplatte', is why they were not launched earlier to split the Allied priorities.

Whatever the Führer's reasons, Ob West issued orders on December 22 to General Hermann Balck's Heeresgruppe G for 'the reconquest of the Saverne gap and the subsequent destruction of the enemy strength in Alsace'. Two days later, while seven divisions were briefly taken out of the line for a rest, Balck himself was replaced by Generaloberst Johannes Blaskowitz, while the CO of First Armee, General der Panzertruppen Otto von Knobelsdorff, was similarly replaced by General der Infanterie Hans von Obstfelder. (The latter had commanded 28 Jäger Division during the campaigns in Poland and France, XXIX Korps in Russia and most recently LXXXVI Korps in France.)

The offensive, codenamed 'Nordwind', was planned on a roughly 30-mile (50km) front southeast

The Jagdpanzer 38(t) Flamm was an adaptation of the Hetzer, mounting a flamethrower in place of the standard 7.5cm gun. Of the ten in 353 Panzer-Flamm Kompanie, which were attached to 17 SS-Panzergrenadier Division, only four survived their first engagement against the U.S. 44th Infantry Division west of Bitche. (U.S. Signal Corps)

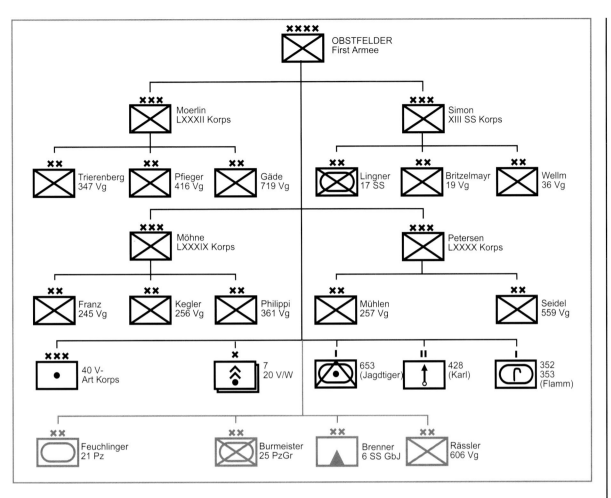

of Saarbrücken with Sarreguemines and Bitche as the initial objectives. This would enable Obstfelder's First Armee to establish a shoulder behind the river Saare while its mobile elements swept south into Alsace towards Strasbourg. At that point, it was planned, General Friedrich Wiese's Nineteenth Armee could break out north from the Colmar pocket to link up with Obstfelder's forces, recapture Strasbourg and, hopefully, entrap a substantial part of Major-General Edward Brooks' U.S. VI and Général de Montsabert's French II Corps.

The forces that could be assembled for 'Nordwind' looked impressive on paper but, in fact, were pitifully weak for their assigned tasks despite the over-extended Allied lines. The spearhead was SS-Gruppenführer Max Simon's XIII SS-Korps, which in addition to the three divisions in the front line on December 31, had 21 Panzer and 25 Panzergrenadier Divisions as a heavy mobile reserve to exploit a breakthrough. Generalleutnant Edgar Feuchtinger's 21 Panzer Division, however, was a mere shadow of the original formation which had wreaked such havoc in North Africa.

Re-formed in 1943 after the final defeat in Tunisia, it was seriously understrength at the time of D-Day but still fought hard in front of Caen and had only been partially rebuilt in time for 'Nordwind'. Oberst Arnold Burmeister's 25 Panzergrenadier Division was in no better shape, having spent three years on the central sector of the Russian front before being transferred to the west, where it fought against Patton's Third Army at Metz and Bitche towards the end of 1944.

Of Simon's other formations, by far the best was Generalmajor August Welln's 36 Volksgrenadier Division. As an infantry division this had fought well in France in 1940 before being motorised for the attack on Russia and later upgraded to a Panzergrenadier division, fighting at Leningrad, Rzhev and Kursk before being virtually destroyed on the river Beresina. Even though now designated a Volksgrenadier division, it still had a far higher allocation of motorised transport than any of the others. SS-Standartenführer Hans Lingner's 17 SS-Panzergrenadier Division 'Götz von Berlichingen' – whose ranks included Belgian volunteers – was a late war formation which had been stationed on the Biscay coast at the time of D-Day.

The Jagdtiger which equipped 653 schwere Panzerjäger Abteilung was an adaptation of the Tiger II with a fixed superstructure mounting a 12.8cm PaK 44 L/55. Its 8-inch (200mm) frontal armour was impervious to any anti-tank gun but the vehicle was not immune to rocket-firing fighters. Only 48 were ever built.
(U.S. Signal Corps)

Rushed from Tours to Normandy, it fought well at Carentan and St Lô, then at Metz. By this time it was down to about 4,000 men and had only been partially rebuilt in time for 'Nordwind'. Generalmajor Karl Britzelmayr's 19 Volksgrenadier Division was in poor shape, having been created from the remnants of 19 Luftwaffen Feld Division and 77 Infanterie Division in August 1944 and rushed from Denmark to take part in the new offensive.

Of the rest, little if anything better can be said. The three Volksgrenadier divisions (347, 416 and 719) in General der Infanterie Moerlein's LXXXII Korps on First Armee's right flank were all composed of elderly reservists recently withdrawn from occupation duties in Denmark and Holland. They had very little artillery and much of it belonged in a museum. The later addition of Generalmajor Hans Degan's tough 2 Gebirgs Division (which had taken part in the invasion of Norway in 1940 and then spent most of the war on the Murmansk front) put some sinew into the Korps, but not enough to produce victory.

The two Volksgrenadier divisions in General der Flieger Petersen's LXXX Korps were in slightly better shape, although Oberst Erich Seidel's 559th had suffered badly against Patton's forces during the earlier battles around Nancy. Finally, on the left flank

of the assault, the three divisions in General der Infanterie Möhne's LXXXIX Korps all had a nucleus of combat veterans, but two of them – 245 and 256 – had incurred heavy losses during the battle of the Scheldt estuary, while 361 had only been partially rebuilt after being virtually destroyed during the Soviet summer offensive. LXXXIX Korps also had SS-Gruppenführer Karl Brenner's 6 SS-Gebirgsjäger Division 'Nord' in reserve, but at the beginning of the offensive only a kampfgruppe under SS-Standartenführer Franz Schreiber had arrived, the rest of the division still being in transit from Norway.

Three unusual formations had been allocated to First Armee for 'Nordwind', but they had little effect on events. The Jagdtigers in 653 schwere Panzerjäger Abteilung were totally unsuited to offensive operations and most rapidly fell easy prey to Allied fighter-bombers. The huge 54cm self-propelled 'Karl' mortars in 428 Mörser Batterie were designed for siege warfare, not blitzkrieg; while the twenty flamethrowing Jagdpanzer 38(t) Hetzers divided between 352 and 353 Panzer-Flamm Kompanien had no defence against Allied tank destroyers. More conventional support for the operation was provided by 410 Volks-Artillerie Korps and 7 and 20 Volks-Werfer Brigaden,

Considering the expenditure of manpower, the gains made by First Armee during Operation 'Nordwind' were extremely modest. The subsequent attacks through Wissembourg and Gambsheim threatened Haguenau but even the arrival of XXXIX Panzer Korps proved insufficient to do more than dent the American and French lines. Similarly, Nineteenth Armee's sortie out of the Colmar pocket never really threatened Strasbourg.

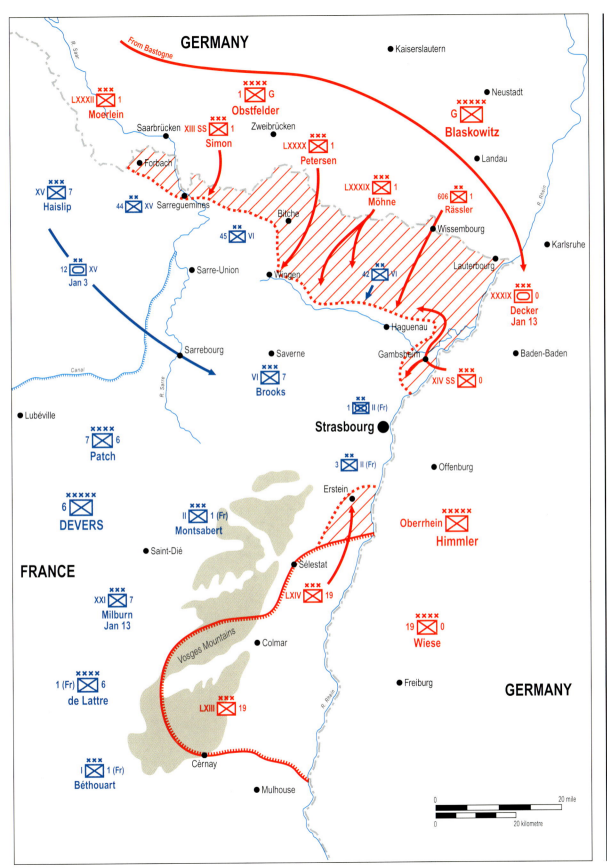

GERMANY

From Bastogne

• Kaiserslautern

LXXXII ☒ 1
Moerlein

1 ☒ G
Obstfelder

• Neustadt

Saarbrücken

XIII SS ☒ 1
Simon

Zweibrücken

LXXXX ☒ 1
Petersen

G ☒
Blaskowitz

• Landau

• Forbach

LXXXIX ☒ 1
Möhne

606 ☒ 1
Rässler

XV ☒ 7
Haislip

44 ☒ XV
Sarreguemines

• Bitche

• Wissembourg

• Karlsruhe

45 ☒ VI

Lauterbourg

R. Rhein

12 ☐ XV
Jan 3

• Sarre-Union

• Wingen

42 ☒ VI

XXXIX ☐ 0
Decker
Jan 13

Canal

R. Sarre

• Sarrebourg

• Saverne

VI ☒ 7
Brooks

• Haguenau

Gambsheim

• Baden-Baden

XIV SS ☒ 0

• Lubéville

1 ☒ II (Fr)

Strasbourg ●

7 ☒ 6
Patch

3 ☒ II (Fr)

• Offenburg

6 ☒
DEVERS

II ☒ 1 (Fr)
Montsabert

Erstein

Oberrhein ☒
Himmler

FRANCE

• Saint-Dié

• Sélestat

XXI ☒ 7
Milburn
Jan 13

LXIV ☒ 19

19 ☒ 0
Wiese

• Colmar

1 (Fr) ☒ 6
de Lattre

Vosges Mountains

• Freiburg

GERMANY

LXIII ☒ 19

I ☒ 1 (Fr)
Béthouart

• Cèrnay

R. Rhein

• Mulhouse

0   20 mile

0   20 kilometre

89

although there was no preliminary artillery barrage.

The attack by XIII SS-Korps broke through the lines of the U.S. 44th Infantry Division (XV Corps) at Sarreguemines, but then faltered because this was just where U.S. intelligence had predicted an assault would come. The attackers were forced back and the CO of 17 SS-Panzergrenadier Division, Hans Lingner, was captured a few days later. The attacks by LXXXX and LXXXXIX Korps on their left were initially more successful, because Allied intelligence had failed to detect their build-up and had interpreted the withdrawal of some of their strength from the front line as a prelude to sending them north to Bastogne. Bitche quickly fell to 559 Volksgrenadier Division and 361 Volksgrenadier Division was soon approaching Wingen, where however, the U.S. 45th Infantry Division (VI Corps) was fighting back hard.

By January 3 XIII SS-Korps, having failed, was back behind its start line, so 21 Panzer and 25 Panzergrenadier Divisions, supposed to have exploited the hoped-for breakthrough northwest of Bitche, were transferred to LXXXX Korps. Next day, Generalleutnant Rudolf Rässler's reserve 606 Volksgrenadier Division launched a supporting

Jagdpanther from 654 schwere Panzerjäger Abteilung disabled by French tanks a few miles east of Colmar during de Lattre's final push to eliminate the pocket. (ECP Armées)

attack through Wissembourg, on First Armee's left flank, but this fell on thin air because the U.S. 42nd Infantry Division opposing it was already pulling back under orders to a new line behind the river Moder. Reinforced by 21 Panzer and 25 Panzergrenadier Divisions, however, 'Gruppe Rässler' was soon threatening the 42nd on the Moder line at Haguenau.

Reichsführer Heinrich Himmler's Heeresgruppe Oberrhein was now brought into play, and on the same day as Rässler's attack, Oberst Erich Löhr's 553 Volksgrenadier Division from XIV SS-Korps assaulted across the Rhein at Gambsheim. Its objective was Strasbourg, which at the time the attack began was actually undefended because the U.S. VI Corps had evacuated the city and the French divisions assigned to its defence had not yet got into position. By January 5, however, both the 1e Division Motorisée and 3e Division Algérien were in position while the newly arrived U.S. 12th Armored Division was assembling to counter-attack.

While these battles were raging north of Strasbourg, the commander of Nineteenth Armee, General Friedrich Wiese, was assembling his own forces for an assault northward out of the Colmar pocket towards Strasbourg, intending to link up with the Gambsheim troops. The forces committed to the attack on January 7, codenamed operation 'Sonnenwende' (Solstice), were Generalmajor Schiel's veteran 198 Infanterie Division, 106 Panzer Brigade

Appearing relieved that for themselves the war is over, cheerful PoWs from Generalmajor Schiel's 198 Infanterie Division, which had been trapped in the Colmar pocket, and Generalmajor Degan's 2 Gebirgs Division at an assembly point in February 1945. (U.S. Army)

and a company of Jagdpanthers from 654 schwere Panzerjäger Abteilung. (The other divisions in Nineteenth Armee were 159, 189, 269 and 338 Infanterie and 16 and 716 Volksgrenadier.) To begin with the operation seemed to be going well, but on the 9th the 3e Division Algérien counter-attacked at Erstein, just south of Strasbourg. The M10 tank destroyers of the 7e Régiment de Chasseurs d'Afrique took a heavy toll and, as elsewhere, the attack floundered to a standstill.

Further north, Generalleutnant Karl Decker's XXXIX Panzer Korps staff had arrived in the Lauterborn sector, transferred from the Bastogne front after the unsuccessful attack at Lutrebois on December 30. Decker now took over temporary command of 'Gruppe Rässler', but on January 13 was re-assigned to Heeresgruppe Oberrhein tasked with breaking out of the Gambsheim bridgehead since 553 Volksgrenadier Division had failed in its attempt to take Strasbourg, although it had reached the outer suburbs. (Its unfortunate CO, Erich Löhr, was later court-martialled on Himmler's orders.) Decker was given two new divisions, SS-Brigadeführer Heinz Harmel's 10 SS-Panzer 'Frundsberg' and Generalleutnant Wolfgang Erdmann's 7 Fallschirm, both of which had earlier fought at Arnhem. Armoured support was provided by 394 Sturmgeschutz and 667 Sturm-Artillerie Brigaden.

The new assault was spearheaded by 10 SS-Panzer Regiment, which, by January 17, had linked up with Rässler's 606 Volksgrenadier Division near Haguenau. However, the understrength U.S. 42nd Infantry Division defending this sector had now been reinforced by the arrival of the 12th Armored and

further progress proved impossible even though, four days later, Ob West telexed OKW with a rather improbable statement that, 'the enemy is withdrawing in Alsace and he will have the time neither to reposition his defences nor to regroup his remaining strength'!

In actual fact the Allies by this time had gone over to the counter-attack, since Eisenhower had ordered the elimination of the Colmar pocket as a necessary prelude to restoring the situation in Alsace. Major-General Frank Milburn's XXI Corps, Seventh Army, had become operational on the 13th with two infantry divisions transferred from First Army in the Ardennes, the 28th and 75th, plus the 3rd, which had been on attachment to the French II Corps. In its place, Général de Montsabert's Corps had been joined by the 5e Division Blindé, giving the Allies four armoured divisions on the Alsace front (French 1e, 2e and 5e and U.S. 12th). II Corps began its attack on the 20th from the north through Sélestat with 2e and 5e Divisions Blindées and 9e Division Coloniale. I Corps simultaneously assaulted from the south through Cernay with 1e Division Blindé, 2e Division Marocain and 4e Division de Montagne, while the U.S. XXI Corps pressed forward in the centre.

The seven remaining depleted divisions of Wiese's LXIII and LXIV Corps fought back gamely but Colmar itself fell on February 2 and within another week the rest of Wiese's men were back east of the Rhine. Similarly, in the north the Gambsheim bridgehead was eliminated, Bitche recaptured and by the end of the month operation 'Nordwind' was nothing but an ignominious memory.

EPILOGUE

WHY 'HERBSTNEBEL' FAILED

The very short and yet unsatisfying answer as to why operation 'Herbstnebel' failed is that it was the pipedream of a lunatic from beginning to end. Gerd von Rundstedt, recalled from retirement to figurehead the operation because it was hoped his appointment would lull the Allies into a sense of complacent security, pinpoints the answer rather more accurately. 'All,' he said, 'absolutely all conditions for the possible success of such an offensive were lacking.'

There is only room here to summarise what he meant, and it must be pointed out that German and American authorities give different priorities to the individual aspects. All agree, however, that it was the failure of the Panzer spearheads to achieve a quick and decisive breakthrough which caused the operation to fail. It is in the reasons for *this* failure that opinions differ. Contributory factors include lack of training or experience in the hastily rebuilt German divisions, poor leadership in certain instances and, on occasion, poor discipline. The initial failure can also be attributed partially to the failure of the pioniere to get the necessary bridges built quickly enough, and the unexpectedly tough opposition from small American units at natural choke points on the rollbahns.

These had a knock-on effect which prevented the Panzers from sustaining the momentum of the advance even once a local breakthrough had been achieved, because the huge traffic jams that inevitably built up in their wake prevented fuel supplies reaching them and hindered the infantry, without whose support tanks cannot operate most effectively. Conversely, where the infantry led the way, their horse-drawn artillery caused its own traffic jam which the Panzers had to struggle to get through.

In general, the German infantry – many of whom were, indeed, untrained and lacked combat experience – performed magnificently. However, their lack of mobility, and the overwhelming superiority of American artillery, proved decisive on far too many occasions. The Volksgrenadiers could not get their guns to the front quickly enough, whereas the fully motorised Americans could move theirs around with ease and suffered from no ammunition shortages. The war of supply – the Materialschlacht – was perhaps the most crucial factor of all in sealing the fate of the offensive.

The same traffic jams on narrow, ice-bound roads edged with often precipitous cliffs and gorges also hampered the deployment of reserves. Held back initially to exploit a breakthrough, the reserves were generally committed willy-nilly at crisis points long after any advantage had already been sacrificed. What the above all boils down to in the end is faulty planning, despite the length of time it took, coupled to faulty intelligence – not so much about Allied dispositions in fact as about the condition of some of the vital bridges, for instance.

This introduces perhaps the final factor in the equation, and some commentators think it the most significant. That is, the failure of the Luftwaffe to provide adequate support. Hermann Göring shrugged afterwards and said, 'it was no longer 1940'. That much is true. The same weather that hindered the Allied tactical air forces also grounded the Jagdstaffeln. But they lacked trained, experienced pilots and when they were unleashed could not cope. If anything postwar studies have proved – and the 1991 Gulf War is a prime example – that a ground offensive is almost certainly doomed to failure unless air superiority is secured and maintained.

By January 3, when the Allied counter-offensive began in earnest, and certainly over the period January 2-5, the Heeresgruppe B perimeter was already shrinking drastically. Except to the immediate southeast of Bastogne, Seventh Armee had been driven back behind its start line; in the north, Sixth Panzer Armee had been forced back well behind the Rur, while in the centre Fifth Panzer Armee's remaining 'bulge' was threatened by assaults from north and south aimed at eliminating it completely at Houffalize.

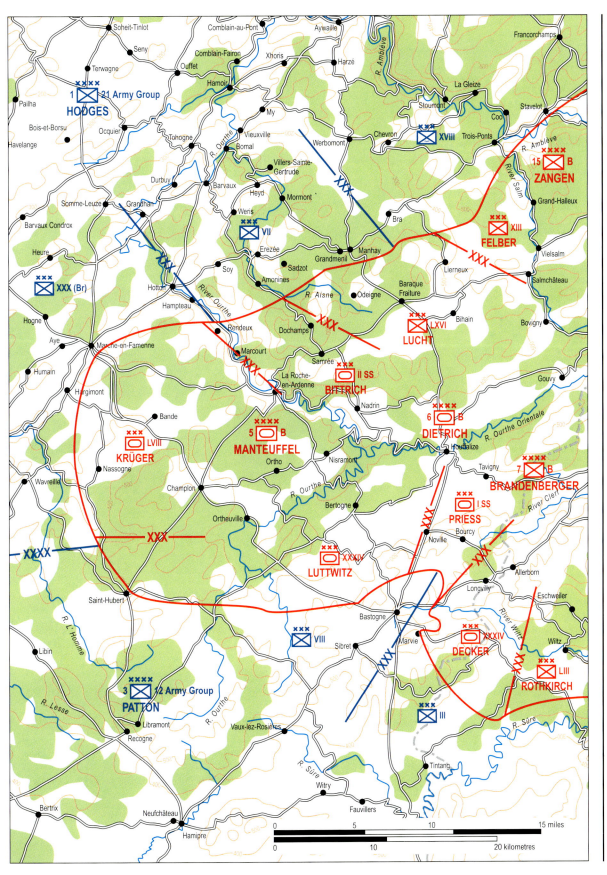

WARGAMING – THE ARDENNES
AXIS SOUTHERN SECTOR

The Ardennes Offensive of December '44 represents the last desperate gasp in the West by a defeated and crippled Germany. Recent anniversaries and commemorations, events in the cinema (as well as the reminiscences of relatives) have brought the war into sharper focus in the public mind with a consequent increase in interest. All these factors make World War II a must for many wargamers. Wargaming with model figures offers the budding general possibly the most visually satisfying medium for refighting World War II battles – particularly the Ardennes Campaign.

Figures and models
Below is a list, by no means comprehensive, of the main figure manufacturers. Many can be obtained from good model shops or the addresses of the individual manufacturers can be found in most wargame magazines.

6-mm /1/300th Scale:
Heroics and Ross
1/285th Scale:
GHQ via Chiltern Miniatures
10-mm/1/200th Scale:
Skytrex
Wargames South

15-mm Scale:
Skytrex
Old Glory
Tin Soldier
20-mm Scale:
SHQ
Skytrex
Platoon 20
Figures Armour and Artillery (FAA)
Wargames Foundry (limited ranges)
Plus many plastic kits by Matchbox, Airfix, Hasagawa, Esci etc …
25mm Scale:
1st Corps
Battle Honours

Computer Games
Empire Interactive's 'Battleground Ardennes'
Microsoft's 'Close Combat –- Normandy to the Ardennes'
Strategic Simulation Inc's 'Panzer General' and 'Steel Panthers III'
Strategic Studies Group's 'Ardennes Offensive'

SELECT BIBLIOGRAPHY

Cole, Hugh M. *The Ardennes: Battle of the Bulge.* United States Army in World War II, Office of the Chief of Military History, Washington D.C., 1965.
Crookenden, Lieutenant-General Sir Napier. *Battle of the Bulge 1944.* Ian Allan, Shepperton, 1980.
Eisenhower, John S. D. *The Bitter Woods.* Robert Hale, London, 1969.
Elstob, Peter. *Hitler's Last Offensive,* Secker & Warburg, London, 1971.
MacDonald, Charles B. *The Battle of the Bulge.* George Weidenfeld & Nicolson, London, 1984.
Marshall, Colonel S. L. A. *Bastogne: The Story of the First Eight Days.* U.S. Army in action series, Center of Military History, Washington D.C., 1946, reprinted 1988.

Nafziger, George F. *The German Order of Battle: Panzers and Artillery in World War II; Infantry in World War II.* Both Greenhill Books, London, and Stackpole Books. PA, 1999.
Pallud, Jean Paul. *Battle of the Bulge Then and Now.* Battle of Britain Prints International, London, 1984.
Parker, Danny S. *Battle of the Bulge.* Greenhill Books, Lionel Leventhal Ltd, London, 1991.
Stanton, Shelby L. *World War II Order of Battle.* Presidio Press, Novato, California, 1984.
Quarrie, Bruce. *Airborne Assault.* Patrick Stephens, Wellingborough, 1991.
Strawson, John. *The Battle for the Ardennes.* B.T. Batsford, London, 1972.
Strong, Major-General Sir Kenneth. *Intelligence at the Top.* Cassell, London, 1968.

INDEX

Figures in **bold** refer to illustrations

COMPANION SERIES FROM OSPREY

ELITE

Detailed information on the uniforms and insignia of the world's most famous military forces. Each 64-page book contains some 50 photographs and diagrams, and 12 pages of full-colour artwork.

NEW VANGUARD

Comprehensive histories of the design, development and operational use of the world's armoured vehicles and artillery. Each 48-page book contains eight pages of full-colour artwork including a detailed cutaway.

WARRIOR

Definitive analysis of the armour, weapons, tactics and motivation of the fighting men of history. Each 64-page book contains cutaways and exploded artwork of the warrior's weapons and armour.

CAMPAIGN

Concise, authoritative accounts of history's decisive military encounters. Each 96-page book contains over 90 illustrations including maps, orders of battle, colour plates, and three-dimensional battle maps.

MEN-AT-ARMS

An unrivalled source of information on the organisation, uniforms and equipment of the world's fighting men, past and present. The series covers hundreds of subjects spanning 5,000 years of history. Each 48-page book includes concise texts packed with specific information, some 40 photos, maps and diagrams, and eight colour plates of uniformed figures.

AIRCRAFT OF THE ACES

Focuses exclusively on the elite pilots of major air campaigns, and includes unique interviews with surviving aces sourced specifically for each volume. Each 96-page volume contains up to 40 specially commissioned artworks, unit listings, new scale plans and the best archival photography available.

COMBAT AIRCRAFT

Technical information from the world's leading aviation writers on the aircraft types flown. Each 96-page volume contains up to 40 specially commissioned artworks, unit listings, new scale plans and the best archival photography available.